A Touchstone for the Tradition

A Touchstone for the
ᴄʀᴀᴅɪᴛɪᴏɴ

THE WILLIE CLANCY SUMMER SCHOOL

Tony Kearns & Barry Taylor

First published in 2003 by
Brandon
an imprint of Mount Eagle Publications
Dingle, Co. Kerry, Ireland

10 9 8 7 6 5 4 3 2 1

ISBN 0 86322 308 7

Mount Eagle Publications receives support from
the Arts Council/An Chomhairle Ealaíon.

Cover design: id communications, Tralee, Co. Kerry
Typesetting by Red Barn Publishing, Skeagh, Skibbereen
Printed by CraftPrint

Acknowledgements

The text and photographs that form the basis for this work originate from two separate projects, both of which were concerned with documenting and analysing the School. In 1992, Tony Kearns commenced the task of building a comprehensive photographic archive; the first exhibition of his photographs was held at the School in 1996 and has been repeated on several occasions. Barry Taylor has been researching various aspects of the School since his first attendance in 1975. In 1988, he completed a thesis on the School for a master's degree (A *Lifeline for the Tradition: The Willie Clancy Summer School*, MA Irish Studies, Bath Spa University College, 1998.) The similarity of the two projects was first observed by Muiris Ó Rócháin, who suggested that, together, they might form the basis for a book.

The authors would like to express their gratitude to the Willie Clancy School community – directors, teachers, administrators, young gophers, students and supporters alike – all of whom have cooperated in the making of this book. Although singling out individuals in this community is difficult, mention must be made of the contributions of Nicholas Carolan, Finbar Boyle, Seamus Mac Mathúna, Liam McNulty, Eamon McGivney, Brid O'Donohue (O'Brien) and Kieran Vaughan.

However, special thanks are due to the School's founding directors, Muiris Ó Rócháin and Harry Hughes, without whose immense support and assistance this book would not have been possible.

Finally, heartfelt thanks to our spouses, Jacqueline and Yanny, for their patience, understanding, assistance and much valued advice throughout the long years of research and preparation that led to this publication.

Pat Mitchell (foreground) with his students, 2001.

Introduction

ULLEANN PIPER, WHISTLE and flute player, singer and storyteller Willie Clancy spent the majority of his life working as a carpenter in Miltown Malbay – a small town located near Ireland's Atlantic coast in the midwest county of Clare. Although Willie was born in Miltown, his family traditions came from the rural communities surrounding Miltown – the true strongholds of the area's musical traditions up to the middle of the twentieth century.

By the time Willie was an adult, these communities were in steep decline. From the generation for whom 'traditional' music, dance and song had formed a natural part of their life, few remained, and many of these were eventually forced to seek a new life away from rural west Clare – a path followed by Willie in 1953.

On his return to Miltown in 1957, the musical renaissance of the 1950s was under way. Willie spent the years of his forties participating in the typical activities of a leading traditional musician of the period: playing in *céilí* bands, giving concert performances, making gramophone records, broadcasting on the radio, while, of course, continuing to sing, play and stay in his community. In a final twist of fate, the last decade of Willie's life was marked by a strong upsurge of interest in the musical culture of rural Ireland – paradoxically, among the youth of urban Ireland. During this period, Willie and many of his contemporaries were 'discovered' by the young enthusiasts, an occurrence that led directly to the founding of the Willie Clancy Summer School, following his tragically early death in 1973.

Just a few months after Willie's passing, some of his friends and musical companions launched the School in Miltown Malbay, and within a decade it had become recognised as Ireland's foremost venue for teaching traditional music. From the beginning, a written constitution, mission statement or even the use of descriptive terms such as 'traditional' or 'music' were considered unnecessary as the name Willie Clancy was a sufficient statement of the founders' intentions. Their vision was clear and simple: to commemorate Willie's life with an event that would enable the musical culture of the local community (and that of the Irish traditional musical community at large) to be passed on to future generations by its practitioners. In 1973, the School was an event that rocked the contemporary traditional music establishment and, even in the twenty-first century, continues to set standards for the study and practice of traditional music.

Our main aim is to present the fullest picture of this unique and exciting event. However, as the 'Willie Week' is a school and not, as often described, a festival, our main concentration is on the teaching aspect. The public lectures, recitals and the informal sessions in the town's streets and bars represent only the tip of the iceberg, and most people visiting Miltown during the week remain unaware of the scope and scale of the School. This includes both the students, who, generally, only sample their individual classes, and the teachers and class administrators who are rarely able to move away from their immediate environment. Therefore, in order to convey some idea of the unique atmosphere of the hundreds of classes scattered in and around Miltown, we have provided a diary to represent a typical week's teaching activity.

While education provides the main focus, we hope also to cast a light on some more general topics. During Willie's life, dramatic changes occurred in Irish society – not least being the birth of the first independent nation state on the island. As in the case of all nations emerging from the shadow of colonial rule, many real and, in some cases, spurious images have been utilised to help bind together the new state. Irish music has not been immune from this practice, and we hope to dispel some widely held myths concerning its role in Irish life, both past and present.

We hope that A *Touchstone for the Tradition* will revive happy memories for past students and visitors and, perhaps more importantly, tempt those have not experienced the event to make the journey to Miltown Malbay.

Barry Taylor and Tony Kearns 2002

Note: For a comprehensive bibliography and discography of Irish music, readers are referred to Fintan Vallely, *The Companion to Irish Traditional Music* (Cork: Cork University Press, 1999). Works referred to in the text are detailed in the relevant footnote.

Monday

I T'S 9.45 A.M. and all the small roads leading St Joseph's Secondary School, Spanish Point, are heavily congested. Nearing St Joseph's, the procession of cars is joined by an ever-increasing tide of pedestrians, most carrying some kind of musical instrument case. The roadside verges and any other vacant areas are littered with cars parked at angles that indicate hasty abandonment. Entering the grounds, the reason is obvious: every parking space has been filled, and the field in front has been commandeered to provide yet more room for the flood of traffic.

From the entrance to the main building, a queue stretches some hundred yards long as students wait to enrol. It's a beautiful sunny morning, and the air of eager expectancy is heightened as new students try to find out what to expect from their more experienced colleagues.

Inside the crowded foyer, a small army of young helpers carries out enrolment. They answer a seemingly endless stream of questions regarding timetables, the format of classes and the availability of places for specific teachers. In the meantime, they try to determine the level of proficiency of individual students – a critical stage in the attempt to place students in the appropriate class. In the heart of the building, a throng of fiddle-case carrying hopefuls have been identified as potential advanced students. From the balcony above, fiddle school director John Kelly is attempting to separate the mass into the groups of twenty or so that will eventually form the week's classes, an ambition continually thwarted by the desire of friends not to be separated.

Eventually the mass begins to thin out as groups disappear into the surrounding classrooms, and before long the noise of the throng is joined by the discordant sound of the many aspirants undergoing assessment by the their teachers. But as soon as the advanced group is dispersed, the space is filled with those at an intermediate level, and so the process continues until every candidate is allocated to a class.

* * *

In Room 14, Armagh-born Brendan McGlinchey has started the process of assessing his group of fifteen or so hopefuls. A small boy, not more than ten years of age, is rattling out a jig on a fiddle that seems disproportionately large. Brendan nods in approval – 'Good boy' – whilst an anxious father hovers in the background and is only finally assured when told that his son can stay in the group. The other members are each invited to play a piece. Two small girls play excellent reels, whilst their friend displays signs of a classical training when playing an air. 'Play me a dance tune,' says Brendan, and the young lady duly obliges. So on round the circle. One woman displays expertise with a fiery performance in the single-bowing style associated with some Donegal fiddle players. 'You know,' says Brendan, 'some people have to learn to play fast and some have to learn to play slow.'

Prospective fiddle students registering for classes, 2001.

At this point the door opens, and two more aspirants are ushered into the room. A man from Boston, Massachusetts, displays a technique and assurance which suggests that the role of teacher might be more appropriate for him. He later explains that he is a classically trained violin player and has come to Miltown to expand his knowledge of traditional fiddle playing. When asked to play by Brendan, one very young girl requests that he should tune her fiddle for her. Brendan patiently obliges, and the girl struggles through her tune; later, Brendan politely recommends that she might benefit from being with less advanced students.

By 11 a.m. everyone has been heard, and the class has settled into some kind of shape. Brendan tells his students: 'I believe that I can help each one of you to improve in some way if you stay with me. But if you think that another class or teacher would be more appropriate, you are free to change. Don't feel any obligation; it's your choice.' No one moves. 'OK, let's try a tune – does anyone know "Kitty's Gone a-Milking"?' Some nod and some shake their heads. Brendan picks up the fiddle and plays the reel, joined by a few students after the opening bars. 'Let's try to break it down into phrases. I'll play the first phrase a few times, and then we'll all try it together.'

After the group has played through the first phrase a few times, Brendan asks class members to play it individually. The first phrase contains a particularly tricky passage that requires a bowed triplet. Brendan explains to the group that there are several different ways of playing a bowed triplet and that he starts on a downstroke. The man from Boston says he was told to always start on an up-bow. Brendan takes his time before replying that this demonstrates the variety of options open to traditional musicians. One by one, the students demonstrate their proficiency on this phrase while Brendan points out individual strengths and weaknesses. 'You're a bit weak in your trebling,' he says to one student, whilst another is advised that his triplets are overemphasised. Although the class is quite large, each student receives individual attention, whilst general points are made for the benefit of all. 'In order to make the most of a tune, it's essential that you're relaxed. It's impossible to play at your best when you're tense. Try to think that you're sitting at home in your chair before the fire.'

With that there's a knock on the door, and the class is informed that it's break time. Brendan smiles and the tension drops.

* * *

Officially, the School does not accept complete beginners for fiddle classes, but it's fairly obvious that a number of the students in Room 4 are comparative novices. Liam O'Connor and Sean McNamara have decided to start the class on a polka, as it is generally thought that polkas are easier to master than jigs, reels and hornpipes. They have distributed the notation for the tune, and this has revealed an immediate problem, as many members of the class are unfamiliar with staff notation. Sean is now faced with the unenviable task of converting the existing material into various notation systems with which he is unfamiliar.

After an hour or so, many have mastered the basic elements of the tune. Liam divides the class into groups of three and asks each group to try the tune: this is a good technique as it doesn't isolate tentative starters but allows the teachers to identify individual problems. Sean picks up some basic faults: 'Try supporting the fiddle between the first finger and thumb of your left hand. If you rest it on your palm, you'll find it very difficult to bring all your fingers into play.' He goes around the group and adjusts the grip of a number of students. A young woman from Japan is advised to be more assertive in her bowing, while a young Irish lad is advised to hold the fiddle up. 'Perhaps you might do better using a shoulder rest,' advises Liam and hands the rest from his own instrument to the lad. It seems to make an immediate improvement, and Liam suggests that the lad buy a rest from the music shop on the main street.

Liam progresses through the individual phrases, and after a time all members of the group are able to follow the complete melody after some fashion. For Liam and Sean, the biggest problem is likely to be the different levels of competence and the number of students in the class. However, this is something they must cope with unless they can find another home for one or two of the more able players.

* * *

Just down the corridor is a class with an entirely different character led by east Clare musician Martin Hayes. Through his many CDs, television and concert performances, Martin's playing has been exposed to a global audience, and to some degree his class is self-selecting, with many students attending over a number of years. Like all the teachers at the School, Martin is committed to imparting as much as possible of the lore of the music and musicians, and as an experienced performer on the concert stage, he is well able to carry out this task. Martin is demonstrating a tune that was played by his father, the late P. Joe Hayes, and is discussing regional styles of music.

'When I was first learning the fiddle, I wasn't aware that some people had classified our music into an east Clare style. I thought that all the musicians

Sean MacNamara (left) and Liam O'Connor, 2001.

I grew up played quite differently, including my father and Paddy Canny, who were neighbours. Paddy was a couple of years older than my father, who learned quite a lot from him, but even so they had quite different ways of playing.' Martin demonstrates the way that P. Joe might have played a tune, followed by a rendition in Paddy Canny's style. 'Strangely, although they had fairly different styles, they could play very well together.'

One young student is asked to play a reel: 'That sounds like a Sligo-type of style,' comments Martin, whereupon the lad confirms that his father is a well-known musician from Sligo. 'You are not all going to be in the position of having such a role model at hand to learn from, and most of you will have to choose a style that you like and are able to play. Although people have tried to say there is an east Clare, most of the people I knew when I was growing up seemed to have different styles, so I had to choose and develop my own method.'

Martin continues to take the group through the tune, using the technique of teaching short phrases favoured by the other teachers. However, unlike many of the other teachers, he does not use any notation system, as he prefers that his students should learn aurally. It is fairly obvious that this class

Martin Hayes (extreme right) and his class, 2001.

contains a high proportion of proficient musicians, and this will allow Martin the opportunity to spend more time discussing wider aspects of the music. During a break in proceedings, Martin asks the class whether they think that this type of discussion is useful, and there are no dissenting voices.

'I think that it's important for you to have a fairly defined aim for this week, and I would like you to tell me what it is. OK, I guess that many of you may not have thought about this in such detail, so perhaps you can have a think overnight, and I'll ask you individually tomorrow.'

At this point, one of Martin's 'regular' students says that he knows what he wants to get out of the week – he wants to master the Tulla Céilí Band's 'swing'. 'I asked you about this last year, and you advised me to listen to Count Basie, so I did, and it did nothing for me.' Martin smiles and nods: 'I'm sorry, but it shows how important it is for you to tell me what you want and, if I fail, then to tell me also. We'll have to think of another way of approaching this.'

Then it's back to the music. Someone asks whether Martin has a tune to go with the one taught earlier. Martin thinks for a minute and then launches into another reel before changing into the first reel. 'I used to play those two regularly together, because the difference in their keys makes for a good change. Many people don't seem to appreciate that playing a tune in a different key completely changes the nature of a tune. A guitar player widely recognised in Irish music circles asked me why I played in different keys, as they couldn't see what difference a key change made. They just put a capo on the guitar and that was it! To me, changing the key can change the whole character of a tune, so I try to play in as many different keys as possible.'

But now it's lunchtime, and the discussion has to end there, no doubt to be carried on for the rest of what promises to be a fascinating week in Room 5.

* * *

Five miles outside Miltown in the Quilty Tavern, dance teachers Aidan Vaughan and Betty McCoy are preparing for another week of hard work, passing on the steps used in dancing the Clare sets. As the hall resounds to the music of the Michael Sexton Céilí Band, sixty students in a circle obediently trot backwards and forwards, the floor clattering to the sound of the basic step. Aidan demonstrates trebbling and brings gasps of admiration – and, in some cases, despair – from his students, many of whom are visiting the country for the first time and will find it hard to follow the lessons. Miltown-born and bred, Aidan tells his students: 'It took me decades to master these skills – I won't say just how many in case I might put you off! So, don't worry if you can't manage them in one morning.' Then, he slows down his rapid feet in order to show the individual movements, but even at this pace many of the students are still puzzled. Aidan and Betty take time out to coach individuals, and Aidan explains that it will be necessary for them to practise for many hours before these steps become an integral part of their dancing armoury.

At the break, a girl from England approaches Aidan and asks if he will take her slowly through the movements so that she can note them: 'I find that I can remember these things better if I write them down.' Aidan smilingly obliges, and then it's time to put some of the practice to the test. The dancers are quickly divided into sets and it's off again.

Pauline from Cork is typical of many of those attending. 'I've been coming to Miltown for more than five years, but previously I've been to accordion classes. This year, I thought I would try to learn some steps. I go regularly to *céilís*, and this should improve my dancing.'

A student from Oregon is making his first visit to Ireland. 'We have a pretty active group in Portland and meet weekly to learn the sets. Generally,

Aidan Vaughan (*centre*), 1992.

we're learning from books, and the end result can be fairly unpredictable. We had a teacher come out from Ireland last year, and he just couldn't believe how we were dancing some of the sets. Many of our group have been to the WCSS, so, as one of leaders, I thought that I should come.'

Dancers in the Clare set class led by Aidan Vaughan and Patrick O'Dea, 1993.

Chapter 1

The Musical Rise of Miltown Malbay

THE MASSIVE IMPROVEMENTS in transportation and communications that have taken place in recent years make it difficult to remember the isolated position of County Clare in earlier times. Visitors jetting into Shannon Airport and taking an air-conditioned coach to the Cliffs of Moher, Bunratty Castle or the rapidly expanding county town of Ennis will find it hard to appreciate the geographic barriers that have made Clare relatively impenetrable to visitors until comparatively recently.[1]

The county is surrounded by water on three of its four sides. Only the north-eastern part of Clare, with its border to County Galway, has a substantial land boundary, and much of that is mountainous. The opening of a branch of the Limerick Junction railway line as far as Ennis in 1858 and the subsequent launch of the West Clare Railway in 1892 opened up the county to some degree. However, rail travellers from Dublin to Ennis had to change at least twice, whilst the West Clare, although picturesque, was noted for its unreliability and eventually closed in 1961.[2] Bus passengers fared no better: to the present day, significant towns such as Miltown Malbay, Feakle and Corofin have only an infrequent bus service.

Within the county, three major upland areas occupy a significant proportion of its territory. Each is of limited agricultural use and none has a history of extensive settlement. But perhaps most significantly for its retention of traditional culture, Clare's hills and mountains made travel and communications difficult.[3]

Historically, the main centres of population have been in four separate areas: the fertile central area extending north from the river Shannon to

Corofin, having Ennis as its focus; an area in the north-east stretching about twenty miles north and west from Lough Dergh; a group of villages on the edge of the Burren in the north-west; and the coastal villages that range along the Shannon estuary and the Atlantic coast. Although these areas are separated by only a few miles, poor communications, natural barriers and varying patterns of agriculture (and fishing in the coastal area) have given each a distinctive culture.

In the first half of the nineteenth century, the population of County Clare grew rapidly from around 208,000 in 1821 to 286,394 by the time of the 1841 census. At that time up to 60 per cent of Clare's dwellings were one-roomed cabins, mostly made from a mud base, mainly in small settlements.

In general, the land is very poor, and the great famines of the 1840s caused misery and hardship. By the time of the 1851 census, 13,438 homes had become uninhabited and the population reduced by 73,996 persons. The economic devastation was immense. In addition to emigration, by 1851 nearly 10 per cent of the population of the county had been forced to seek accommodation in workhouses.[4]

The establishment of the Irish Free State in 1922 failed to halt population decline, and Clare and the other western counties were particularly badly affected. Some degree of economic revival in Ireland from the late fifties helped to stanch the flow of emigration, and by 1991 the population of County Clare had stabilised at an estimated 90,918, 65 per cent of whom were living in rural areas. The increased prosperity of the 1990s (the much vaunted Celtic Tiger) has seen the population rise further to 101,266. However, the majority of that rise has occurred in the traditionally more prosperous central and eastern area, which includes the town of Ennis, while the lowly populated west has continued to decline.[5]

Prior to the great famines, the vast majority of the population of the countryside subsisted off fairly small portions of land (which were progressively sub-divided) held in tenancy – often to an absentee landlord. Successive failures of the potato crop prompted ever-increasing levels of emigration, and as the rural population fell, the process of land sub-division began to decline.[6] Through the latter half of the nineteenth century, political agitation for land reform prompted a number of changes to the longstanding landlord/tenant relationship, culminating in the Land Acts of 1923. The three-quarters of a century following the famine years of the 1840s saw the peasant farmers transformed, first into tenant farmers and, finally, into the owner-occupiers of their own holdings.[7]

As the size of holdings gradually increased, farms began to produce a surplus that might be sold on the open market. Thus, in the last half of the nineteenth century, farmers and townspeople increasingly met at marts and fairs. This helps to explain how English-language songs (published on printed sheets and sold at fairs and markets), dance forms such as the quadrille and new dance tunes were able to make their way into even the remotest parts of the countryside.

* * *

Although located a couple of miles inland, Miltown Malbay belongs to the group of coastal villages scattered along the Atlantic coast and is situated about midway from the mouth of the Shannon to the edge of the Burren. The most direct route from Ennis leads west over Sliabh Callan, and even on today's metalled highway, the mountain can present a formidable obstacle in bad weather. It is not difficult to imagine that, when travel was more commonly accomplished by horse or bicycle, even the most ardent traveller would need a fairly good reason to make the 'trip over the mountain'.

For most of today's visitors, their first view of Miltown and the surrounding coastal plain is from the mountain, and on a fine day it is an impressive sight. Having crested the summit, the road sweeps down to intersect Miltown's main street before continuing on towards Spanish Point.

The earliest inhabitants of Miltown seem to have lived a half-mile or so further to the north of this intersection, in the area between the parish church and the former railway station, where a stone fort (An Chathair) was located. According to local historian Seosamh Mac Mathúna, this is the derivation of the town's Irish name of Sraid na Cathrach (Street of the Fort).[8] The 'Malbay' part of its English name refers to its connection to the nearby coast. Miltown Malbay and the nearby resort of Spanish Point have developed in tandem over the last 250 years, initially under of the influence of the Morony family, who were settled in the south of Clare by the earl of Thomond after the Treaty of Limerick in 1691. In 1750, Edmond Morony acquired lands around the area between Spanish Point and present day Miltown and gradually began to develop the area. In the late eighteenth century, a family house was started at Spanish Point, which later became the home of a community of the Sisters of Mercy and now forms part of the local secondary school.

The Moronys encouraged the development of both the areas around Spanish Point and of Miltown Malbay and were the inspiration for many of the business properties that were built in the town between 1820 and 1860. Early development came where the old road from Inagh (the Ballard road) passes on its way to the coast – an area now known as Canada Cross – and around the Ennis road intersection. Little by little, the intervening space was filled in to form the main street of the village of Miltown Malbay. It is part of its charm that, in a rapidly changing world, the basic structure of Miltown Malbay has altered but little over the last 150 years.

In the 1841 census, Miltown had 213 houses, with a population of 1,452. However, by the middle of twentieth century the population of Miltown had been reduced to 700. The prosperity of the area has certainly increased in recent years – in no small measure due to the influence of the Willie Clancy Summer School – and the population is now estimated to be around 1,200.

Although the scattered *clachans*[9] were the heartland of west Clare's musical tradition, the music, dance and song associated with the countryside also reached into towns such as Miltown. Like many similar country towns in Ireland, Miltown provided a wide range of services for the surrounding rural communities, including markets, fairs, shops, postal services, doctors, etc. In addition, over the years, many country dwellers moved into the town, in the process bringing their traditions with them. The families of many of the best-known traditional musicians, singers and dancers associated with Miltown, including Willie Clancy himself, originated in the surrounding countryside.

The practice of house dancing – the focus of much of the musical and general social activity of the countryside – did not flourish in the town, where it faced competition from entertainments largely contrived for commercial gain, as well as opposition from a powerful clergy.[10] In 1935, in a move that might be thought of as the victory of town over country, the government enacted a law, the Public Dance Halls Act, to prohibit dancing in unlicensed premises. Whether the homely country house dance was intended to fall into the scope of the act is open to debate. However, the local clergy and gardaí certainly acted as if it were and moved rapidly against any unlicensed dance. The period was remembered vividly by fiddle player Junior Crehan:

> So, they barred the country house dance, and the priests was erecting parish halls. All they wanted was to make money – and they got 3d into every shilling tax out of the tickets to pay the government for tax. So the country house dance was knocked out then, and 'twas fox-trots, and big old bands coming down, and our type – we'd be in a foreign country then. We couldn't put up with it at all, the noise and the microphones, and jazz and so on . . . the music nearly died out altogether – Irish music. Then the emigration started. A lot of lads I used to play with went off to England and America, and there was no one but myself

. . . and I used to go down the road, and . . . Honest to God, I used to nearly cry. Nowhere to go – no one to meet, no sets in the houses, nothing left but the hall![11]

As the country house dance began its steady decline, first the clergy and, later, commercial interests moved in to fill the vacuum. In the thirties, parish halls and small commercial ventures were popular venues for dances, but with the outbreak of 'dancing fever' in the 1940s and fifties, large commercial halls, and in summer marquees, took centre stage.

However, there were occasions when traditional music and song could be heard in Miltown. For example, itinerant singers and musicians were always in regular attendance on market days and the horse races held at Spanish Point. In addition, regular *feiseanna* were held on the local football field during the summer months, with country musicians always to the fore. Finally, the launch of the local *Comhaltas Ceoltóirí Éireann* branch and the founding of the Laichtín Naofa Céilí Band provided a much-needed, but relatively short-lived, boost for traditional music in the town, with the organisation of the first county *fleadh cheoil* in 1957 a notable event in its musical history.

Willie Clancy was born in Miltown Malbay on Christmas Eve, 1918. Willie's father, Gilbert, an excellent flute and concertina player, hailed from Islandbawn, a townland four miles or so from Miltown, while his mother, Eileen Killeen from Ennistymon, was a noted singer and concertina player.

The Clancy house in Islandbawn had been a haven for traditional music and was a regular halting place for the blind piper Garrett Barry, who was born in Inagh in 1847 and who, in spite of his expertise and unsurpassed reputation, died in the Ennistymon workhouse in 1899 and was buried in an unmarked pauper's grave in Inagh, where a headstone was erected in 1999.

Barry was also a regular visitor to Caherduff House, just outside Miltown Malbay, which was the home of Junior Crehan's grandparents. His paternal grandmother, Bridget, was a cousin of Barry's, and Junior learned some of Barry's tunes from her lilting. Like many other people in west Clare, Junior had inherited a fund of stories about the piper:

Garret Barry was a blind piper and he was born in Inagh. He was blind since he was four years old with chicken pox. And he used travel around to all the towns and villages and people loved him, he was a lovely musician, and they'd keep him for a week. And then he'd go to the country houses and the country pubs, from Mullagh over to Carthy's in Cloonlaheen. He'd be well looked after everywhere he went. But he'd sit on the little battlement of this bridge and he'd play tunes. But he had one hornpipe that he liked. He'd open with that and he'd finish with that. And people would stand listening. Whatever work they were doing they would stand listening to the music. And some of them picked up the hornpipe. And the name they called it was *Sruthán na gCat*, 'The Stream of the Cat'.[12]

Another man with strong memories of Garrett Barry was Jack O'Donoghue of Stoney village, which is about a quarter of a mile from Barry's birthplace of Kylea, Inagh. According to Jack O'Donoghue, Barry was apprenticed in his youth to a master piper in Kerry, where he displayed a prodigious talent for music.[13] However, according to Willie Clancy: '[Barry] was apprenticed to Frank Cleary, a Limerick piper, who lived in Ennis. Local lore had it that Frank did not give all he should have to his pupil. Maybe it was jealousy; he might have realised that the pupil had more talent than himself. How far this is true is another matter. Local gossip always builds up the local legend.'[14]

Whichever version is correct, Barry subsequently returned to west Clare, where he was to remain for the rest of his life.

Sadly for posterity, Barry was born just before the age of recording, but his music has left an indelible mark on the musical tradition of west Clare. Thanks mainly to the devotion of his friend Gilbert Clancy and, later, Gilbert's son Willie, some of Barry's music has been preserved. Although Gilbert never mastered the pipes, he was able to pick up Barry's music on the flute, and it was on this instrument that Willie first brought out the music of the legendary piper.

Willie Clancy (photo: Mick O'Connor).

There was at least one other piper in the area contemporary to Garrett Barry. John Carroll was a farmer who lived at Freagh, just a couple of miles out of Miltown off the road to Lahinch and within two or three miles of the Clancy household. John and his brother Michael, both well-respected exponents of the concert flute, were well acquainted with Garrett Barry. John's elder brother Martin was the local representative of Scottish Laboratories, a company who purchased kelp for the manufacture of iodine, and his business often took him to Kilrush. Just outside Kilrush, at Knockerra, lived the Moloney brothers, Andrew and Thomas, who had fashioned a set of pipes in the 1830s for the son of a local landowner, Mr Vandeleur. They were never taken up by young Vandeleur, and Martin Carroll eventually purchased the pipes from the Moloney brothers for his younger brother. It is said that John Carroll rapidly mastered the instrument, as did his friend Pat Burke of Miltown Malbay. Burke's father-in-law, Tom Hehir of Feighruisk, in the parish of Connolly, was also an excellent piper, and it appears that Barry, Carroll, Burke and Hehir spent many an evening together.

John Carroll died shortly after Garrett Barry in 1900, and as none of the family had taken up the pipes, they were locked away. Six years later, piper Donncadh Ó Laoire, from near Ballyvourney, County Cork, an organiser for *Conradh na Gaeilge* (the Gaelic League), purchased the pipes from Mrs Carroll for £12. It is thought that the Moloney pipes in the National Museum, Dublin, are these pipes.[15]

With pipers such a scarcity in west Clare, Willie Clancy probably did not hear the sound of the *uilleann* pipes until 1936. The sand hills around Spanish Point were the venue for regular horse racing meetings, and the

A *youthful Willie Clancy* (Irish Traditional Music Archive).

attendant crowds naturally attracted a wide range of merchants, each vying with the other to sell their wares. On one such occasion, the young Willie Clancy and his close friend Martin Talty were making their way towards the races when the sound of travelling piper Johnny Doran could be heard above the noisy crowd:

> We heard the pipes playing as we were coming down the street and we started to run. There was Johnnie Doran, the first time we ever laid eyes on him. We stuck with him all day and in the evening went out to where he was staying, a mile or two beyond Quilty. After that, we went out to him every evening. Later, when he moved on to Kilrush, we went with him. We borrowed two bicycles and bought an old tent. Things were going grand until, one night, a horse walked into the side of it and put his foot through the roof – we finished up in Doran's tent that night![16]

For the musical futures of both Willie and Martin, the die was cast. In 1938, Willie obtained a bag, bellows and chanter from Johnny's piping brother, Felix, commenting, 'I thought I'd won the sweepstake the night I got that!'[17] There is no doubt that in Johnny Doran, Willie Clancy had found his inspiration, and the relationship between the master piper and his young pupil echoed that of Garrett Barry and the young Gilbert Clancy, except that Gilbert was never in a position to emulate Garrett as a piper, due to the lack of a suitable instrument.

Junior Crehan remembered the close relationship between Willie and Johnny Doran:

> As a direct result of listening to Johnny Doran, Willie Clancy took up the *uilleann* pipes. He got his first set from Johnny's brother, Felix. Arra! It was an old battered bag and chanter but poor Willie was delighted to get it. He followed Doran a lot and I suppose Doran gave him a good few tips because Willie used to be in the caravan with him day and night. I remember to break a bolt on the mowing machine and I untackled the horse and went to Miltown on a bicycle to get a new bolt.
>
> Up from the Crosses of Annagh there was a kind of a little bit of commonage and Doran was set up there. There was Willie sitting on the steps going up to the caravan and Doran sitting up higher and they having a set of pipes each. And my trouble was to have that strip of hay cut before nightfall.
>
> I laughed and said – 'Fine it is for you, Willie, that the hay doesn't bother you, or the cows or anything.'[18]

Willie had also followed his father's trade and was a skilled carpenter – a great asset in maintaining such a complex instrument – but music was always Willie's first love. He was a phenomenally quick learner, and he rapidly set about mastering the pipes. During the early days, Gilbert was always ready to advise on the setting of a tune and to point out ways in which Barry had added lustre to his playing. Willie also had access to another first-hand source of the piper's music.

Hugh McCurtin of nearby Clohanbeg was a talented musician on several instruments, including fiddle, concertina, pipes, tin whistle and concert flute. Gilbert Clancy was a close friend of Hugh McCurtin, and they often travelled together to Markham's Cross to meet up with fiddle player Junior Crehan.[19] The house of the McCurtin family, who could trace their ancestry back to the bardic poets of Clare, had been another of Barry's favourite stopping points. During such visits, Barry had played on McCurtin's pipes – another set made by the Moloney Brothers – and these eventually passed to Willie, who treasured them for their Clare connection.

Another musical connection, although initially remote, was with Martin Rochford of Bodyke in distant east Clare. Like Willie, Martin had served his musical apprenticeship on other instruments: in his case, the fiddle and tin whistle. Like Willie, he had long been keen to learn the pipes, and his mind was made up when he heard Tony Rainey, a travelling piper, playing on a market day in 1936 in Ennis. Shortly afterwards, Johnny Doran made

Johnny Doran (right), with Pat Cash and son (Na Píobairí Uilleann).

his first visit to Bodyke, and Martin was able to purchase a set of pipes that Doran had sold to Dan McMahon of Ennis. At around the same time, Martin first met Sean Reid, who had been recently appointed as an engineer with the Clare County Council. Reid was both a keen piper and an enthusiast for all aspects of traditional music, and through him Martin was to meet Willie Clancy. By late 1939, Reid and Rochford were regular visitors to Miltown. At the time Gilbert Clancy was still alive, and so, through his flute playing, Martin Rochford was also able to become acquainted with the piping style of Garrett Barry. Although reunions between Martin and Willie were rare after the late forties, their early meetings had a significant influence on the piping of both men.[20]

The forties and early fifties did not herald good times for the people of rural Ireland. The social historian Terence Brown characterises the period from the early thirties to the late fifties as one of 'stagnation and crisis'.[21] During and following the Second World War (the 'Emergency'), economic and social conditions in Ireland, particularly in the West, were in steep decline. Unlike virtually every other country in Europe, Ireland did not experience a post-war economic boom. *The Irish Times* commented in 1952:

> Housing conditions in rural Ireland. . . remain at a low standard. . . The amenities within most small farms and agricultural workers' houses are, in general, much the same as they were when the land was tilled with a spade and men threshed with a flail. . . Is it surprising that young girls, who are well aware that we live in a world where labour-saving devices hold pride of place, are unwilling to marry into conditions such as they are?[22]

Junior Crehan summed up the feelings of many a musician: 'In the '40's, the rate of emigration increased rapidly. The youth saw nothing in their own country but poverty. . . The countryside was once more going through that terrible silence which it had suffered after the famine – the silence of a departing people and a dying of music and song. These were, indeed, the black Forties.'[23]

But even in these difficult times, there were opportunities for music, dance and song. People remembered Willie Clancy as 'a tall curly-haired lad, invariably accompanied by Martin Talty, at every house dance, wedding, wren dance and American wake in the seven parishes'.[24] He learned step dancing from dancing master Thady Casey, who had danced barefoot to Garret Barry's playing as a young boy, and fiddle from Thady's cousin, Scully Casey of Annagh.[25] According to Pat Mitchell, Willie incorporated much of Scully's fiddle ornamentation into his flute playing and, later on, into his piping. Willie's connection the Casey family was to last for the rest of his life as a result of his friendship with Scully's talented fiddle-playing son Bobby.

Around 1948, through his close friendship with Sean Reid, Willie enjoyed a short spell with east Clare's Tulla Céilí Band, as did both Martin Talty and Bobby Casey. Although some have been quick to dismiss *céilí* bands as an insult to the tradition, without *céilí* bands, there might have been little traditional music left by the 1960s. In any event, the musicians voted with their feet, as even the most cursory glance at the line-up of any of the bands of the 1950s and sixties shows.[26]

Whatever his musical outlet, Willie's favoured instrument remained the pipes, and in 1947 his efforts were rewarded when he took first prize at the *Oireachtas* in Dublin. In 1951, he went to work in Dublin and joined the Leo Rowsome Quartet, along with Sean Seery, Tommy Reck and, sometimes, Leon Rowsome. Dublin was home to many fine musicians, and Willie was able to enjoy the company of fellow Clareman John Kelly, as well as Andy Conroy, Bill Harte, Sonny Brogan and John Potts.

Bobby Casey joined Willie in Dublin for a short period, but in 1953 he left for London, where he was to spend most of his adult life. Soon afterwards, Willie followed, but he never really settled in the 'big smoke', and following the death of his father Gilbert in 1957, he returned to Miltown Malbay. Although Willie's stay in London was short, his playing at that time was featured on a release by the Topic Record Company – perhaps, the first solo commercial recording to be made by a Clare-born traditional musician.[27]

* * *

By the time Willie returned to Miltown, traditional music was on the march in Ireland. Better late than never, Radio Éireann had discovered that there were rich musical pickings to be had in the isolated western regions. In addition, the founding of *Comhaltas Ceoltóirí Éireann* or CCÉ (the Music Association of Ireland) in 1951 and the subsequent launch of its annual *fleadh cheoil* (music festival) provided a major boost for musicians who had laboured for long in isolation. Many new *céilí* bands were launched during this period, prompted by the enthusiasm of the audiences for the band competition held at the *fleadh cheoil*, and usually based around individual branches of CCÉ. Typical of these was the Laichtín Naofa Céilí Band, whose members hailed from the Miltown-Mullagh area. On his return to Miltown, Willie Clancy became an enthusiastic member of the Laichtín Naofa and can be heard playing the pipes on their only commercial recording.[28]

However, County Clare musicians were still known only to a small cognoscenti of traditional music enthusiasts outside of the county. They had not featured in the recording boom of the twenties and thirties and had appeared only rarely on national radio. But when Ciarán Mac Mathúna made the first of his many visits to record traditional musicians for Radio Éireann in 1955, he was to unearth a rich vein of musical genius. The recordings made at this time subsequently provided the foundation for groundbreaking programmes such as A *Job of Journeywork* and *Ceolta Tíre* – the first regular broadcasts of traditional music on the Irish station. The popularity of these programmes, and Mac Mathúna's predilection for the music of the Banner County, served to introduce Clare music to a wider audience, and musicians such as Paddy Canny, Mrs Crotty and Willie Clancy rapidly became household names throughout the country.

Clare's musical reputation was further enhanced with the release in 1956 of a series of 78-rpm recordings by the Tulla Céilí Band, the first major commercial recordings of traditional music to be made in Ireland since the thirties. In the same year, the *Fleadh Cheoil na hÉireann* made its way to Ennis. A year later, the first county *fleadh cheoil* was launched in Miltown Malbay.

As Séamus Mac Mathúna describes:

What with the *Fleadh Cheoil an Chlair* [County Clare Fleadh] at August weekend and the inevitable winding-up sessions in Miltown on the

Bobby Casey, Miltown Malbay, 1975 (photo: Liam McNulty).

following Tuesday, Wednesday and Thursday, it became the highlight of the year for many musicians from Dublin and other parts, rivalling *Fleadh Cheoil na h-Eireann* in musical intensity and atmosphere . . . Thomas O Friel's backroom |a Miltown pub noted for its welcome for musicians| saw some great sessions.[29]

In the 1950s, pub sessions were something new, and their arrival marked the start of an era that, eventually, saw the pub replace the country house as the centre of musical life for the rural community. Although the country house dance flourished only from around the 1870s to the late 1930s, nevertheless, for many country folk, it epitomised the Golden Age of Irish music: '|It was| the centre of activity in those days. It was not only a place of entertainment, it was also a school where the traditions of music-making, storytelling and dancing were passed on from one generation to the next.'[30]

Up to the 1940s, the country house dance was the chief form of entertainment for country people, and set dances were their main feature. In the early years of the twentieth century, transport was limited. The horse and trap were mainly used for business, and for the young people, five miles by foot over poor roads or boggy countryside was a major outing. The increasing availability of the bicycle, however, made venturing further from home an option. The scattered townlands like those surrounding Miltown – such as Ballyvaskin, Caherush, Clohanbeg, Letterkelly, Knockliscrane, Caherogan, Caherduff and Glandine – were the hotbeds of the tradition. During the twenties and thirties, houses such as that of the great singer Tom Lenihan of Knockbrack could attract visitors from as far afield as Mullagh and Quilty.

In the 1950s, the new interest in traditional music and dance prompted at least one revival of the country house dance. Marty Malley of Clohanmore, later a keen supporter of the School, commenced his one-man effort in 1959, and from then until 1972 dances occurred as regularly as ten times a year at his house. In the 1960s,when Marty's native townland had been decimated by emigration, his home became the focal point for different generations of musicians and dancers: not only neighbours, but people from all parts of Ireland, the UK and even the USA.

Willie Clancy was a regular and enthusiastic guest, as Marty remembers: 'One night and a storm blowing: inside, a dance |is| in full swing. At 12 o'clock, the door opening and Willie Clancy, accompanied by Séamus Ennis, rolling in a barrel of porter!'[31]

With the coming of the *fleadh* and the pub session, small towns such as Miltown increasingly became the centre for the musical activities of the surrounding countryside. Before the late 1950s, a fine summer's day in rural Clare would find pubs empty, with local people at work in the bog or at the hay, but as people flocked to the *fleadhs*, it became the norm to wander into a pub during the day and find a session in full swing.

The older musicians were being recognised by a generation of newcomers, and as the rediscovery of the musical traditions of Ireland gathered pace, County Clare became the place to be. In Miltown Malbay, bars such as Friel's, Queally's and Marrinan's were packed with crowds seeking traditional music. Among the more celebrated visitors was the great piper Séamus Ennis, whose duets with Willie in Friel's and Queally's kitchen are legendary.[32]

Although traditional music could be said to be back on the agenda, during the fifties and sixties most of the musicians were from the previous era, and there were relatively few playing opportunities for young people, particularly in the rural areas. However, a couple of miles outside Miltown, Tessie Walsh, a teacher in the national school at Annagh, was ensuring that at least one group of youngsters would be able to preserve the traditions of their locality.

Ciarán Mac Mathúna (standing), with musicians Jimmy Ward, Junior Crehan and Willie Clancy with friends, late 1960s (ITMA).

Among the Welsh family of Mount Scott, local traditions had been zealously preserved. Tessie's father, Paddy, played concertina and whistle, and her mother was a dancer. Her brother, J.C. Welsh, is remembered both as a singer and for his extrovert character. Sister Johanna ('Cissy') inherited her mother's ability as a dancer and was to marry Junior Crehan. Tessie herself played whistle and piano and was church organist in Mullagh for forty years.[33]

Each morning before the official lessons began, Tessie encouraged her class to learn the whistle, and no one was keener to learn than the young Brid O'Donohue:

> I suppose I was six or seven, like all the ones in the first class – everyone got that chance. . . There were four or five of us that, once we got over the marches, got into playing jigs and reels. By the time we were fifth class, we were playing lots of reels and jigs, lovely ones that you wouldn't hear too much of now. . . It was like having a session every morning, and there was no such thing as formal classes. You just went in, and because we were walking to school, we'd be in earlier, and she'd give you the first quarter of an hour in the morning just to play. It never felt like learning![34]

Seamus Ennis (right) and Breandán Breathnach at the piping recital, 1977 (photo: Liam McNulty).

Tessie Welsh had learned dances such as the Caledonian, the plain set and even the comparatively rare Orange and Green early in her life, and later taught them to her pupils. Brid's recollections recall P.W. Joyce's memories of his schooldays in Galbally, County Limerick, a century or so previously: 'Some dozen or more of the scholars were always in attendance in the mornings half an hour or so before the arrival of the master . . . and then, out came the fife and they cleared the floor for a dance. . .'[35]

Brid was born in 1961 in Caherush, midway between Miltown and Quilty. Although neither of her parents played music, both liked 'lively hearty music for a set', while Brid's father Paddy was particularly fond of singing. As a girl, Brid was surrounded by music: mother Evie was a sister of pipe and flute player J.C. Talty. Just down the road were the Sextons: Michael Joe, who played the pipes, and his daughter Mary Anne, who, as Brid put it, 'played a bit on nearly every instrument but was known for the accordion'. Mary Anne was also an excellent whistle player, and once the young Brid had mastered the basics, she was able to pick up Mary Anne's tunes.

Brid remembers playing with flute and whistle luminaries John Fennell and Joe Cuneen on occasional trips to Quilty. Musical visitors were not uncommon in the O'Donohue house. Paddy had been a classmate of Bobby Casey, and Brid remembers sharing a few tunes with the eminent fiddler from nearby Annagh. On another occasion, banjo player Pat Costelloe called, and Brid recalls trying to bring out some tunes with Pat on a toy melodeon that had arrived from Santy.

However, in the late sixties and early seventies, opportunities for a young girl to play music were fairly restricted. With the house dance long gone and at a time when relatively few women in rural Ireland were regular pub goers, this new venue for traditional music was not deemed suitable for a girl not even in her teens. Brid was lucky to be able to hone her skills within the family.

I always wanted to play the flute. I always spent every Sunday inside at [my Uncle] J.C.'s, and he'd give me a chance on the flute – he used to give me an hour on the flute. He'd play the pipes and flute, and every time he stopped up the pipes, I'd have to turn the bag upside down, put a knot in the neck so you couldn't get the air coming out. But I loved the feel of it – it made me feel as if I was actually playing them!

My memories of Willie Clancy were of going into his house. His sister Mary was married to my grand-uncle, Joey Woolf – they lived down the road at home in another house where there was lots of singing.

Because of this, there was a family connection, and my memories of Willie Clancy were never in the pub – I never met Willie Clancy in a pub – but I would have lovely memories of going into his house and playing inside with him in his house. I remember him bringing me out lots of times to the workshop down at the back and making the reeds and all that. . . . He'd ask me what I'd learnt at school, and when I was playing it he might say, 'Play that again now and I'll show you a roll. Put it in there, it'll sound lovely!'[36]

* * *

Around the time that the young Brid O'Donohue was receiving her whistle 'lessons' from Willie Clancy, a young teacher named Helen Brennan had joined the staff at the Spanish Point secondary school. At the request of Breandán Breathnach, Helen began to make regular visits to Miltown to carry out research for him on dancing for a book he was writing.[37] She quickly found that Willie Clancy was a marvellous source: 'Willie was a wonderful raconteur and he had many's the wry and witty comment on the world at large.'[38]

Brid O'Donoghue playing in the whistle recital, 1978 (photo: Liam McNulty).

But Helen was only one of a number of young enthusiasts who were finding Miltown Malbay an inspirational place for aspiring traditional musicians and dancers. Finbar Boyle, a fine singer and one of the leading figures in the folk song 'movement' of the sixties and seventies, remembers:

I was late teens or maybe early twenties when I started going to Miltown Malbay first. I was going there before the School really started at all, initially because Willie Clancy was there. Now I never really knew him, but I was in his presence once or twice in Miltown. I think the word had gone out among all the musicians, and all the people I knew, this was a nice man that knew a lot about music and also, unlike a lot of musicians today, he wasn't adverse to singing a song. . . . I found the whole atmosphere in Miltown at that time was so nice, people were so kind, and there didn't seem to be any great division between the generations. It was fairly common for us in those days to finish work on a Friday evening and to hop on a bus and be in Clare, in Miltown, at 11 o'clock that night. [We would] put up a tent, stay there, and get back to work for Monday morning. . . The hospitality was unbelievable. We often went into Friel's with tents on our backs and were told not to bother, to go upstairs, get two or three of us into a bed, and we'd get our breakfast the next morning – maybe your dinner the next day![39]

In the early seventies, Miltown attracted two young men who were to leave a lasting impression on both the area and, through their efforts on behalf of the local traditions, on the world of Irish music in general. The two were Muiris Ó Rócháin and Harry Hughes, both of whom had recently graduated as teachers. They secured teaching posts in St Joseph's Secondary School, Spanish Point, in 1970 and 1969 respectively, thus beginning a friendship and collaboration that continues to the present day.

In many respects, Muiris Ó Rócháin (b. 1944) and Harry Hughes (b. 1946) were typical of the young people involved in traditional music in the late sixties and early seventies. While neither was a musician, both had been surrounded by traditional culture during their early lives. The Ó Rócháin family pub in John Street, Dingle, County Kerry, was the centre of a long-surviving Wren Day tradition.[40] Following graduation from the University of Cork, Muiris:

. . . went down to South Kerry to the Caherciveen area to teach. But not so much teaching really, as in the area, the last of the great Gaelic speakers was still alive. I started collecting folklore there, out of love for it myself. I gave two years, two winters, collecting very extensively, and I gave my tapes to the Folklore Department at UCD. . . I lived after that in Dublin and three years I was teaching there… At the time in Dublin, John Kelly [senior] was holding court in Donoghue's, and Breandán Breathnach was going to publish his first collection of music . . . I loved the music scene. I met many of the good musicians, and I got friendly with a lot of these people.[41]

Harry Hughes' father played the accordion in the local *céilí* bands of his hometown of Foxford, County Mayo. Although Hughes did not directly follow in his father's footsteps, he inherited his deep interest in traditional music and had assisted both in the organisation of county, provincial and national *fleadhanna*. From childhood, as Hughes says:

I would have been aware of Mrs Crotty, who I knew was from County Clare, and I would have been aware that she was from Kilrush after

Muiris Ó Rócháin, Harry Hughes, Junior Crehan and Canon Mullen (Miltown's parish priest), awaiting President Mary Robinson's arrival to officially open the School in 1993.

hearing Ciarán Mac Mathúna's programme, very, very aware of that. I would have been aware that Garrett Barry was associated with Clare. Again, a lot of it would have been through Ciarán Mac Mathúna's programmes. . . I would have heard of Willie Clancy, too, and now hearing of Willie Clancy would have been through the same medium because that programme was always on in our house. . . So I would have been aware that Clare was a centre of traditionalists, certainly would have been aware. . .[42]

Ó Róchain and Hughes found an affinity with those pubs where music was played. Chief of these was Tom and Maisie Friel's, which might be described as the epicentre of traditional music in Miltown from the late fifties to recent times. It was also one of the main public venues for Willie Clancy in his later years, as Muiris Ó Róchain recalls: 'I came here then in 1970, and naturally enough the people who I met were Willie Clancy, Martin Talty, J.C. Talty – Bobby Casey, who I remembered coming home from England . . . I was very involved, had a very deep interest in music and the culture and language as well.'[43]

Through their friendship with Willie Clancy, Ó Róchain and Hughes were in a good position to observe his effect on the many young enthusiasts visiting Miltown. They also saw how their arrival provided a shot in the arm for local musicians and music devotees. Whether it was the local tradition bearers such as young Brid O'Donohue or those from further afield such as Finbar Boyle, in the midst of so much that was new and exciting for the younger generation, Willie Clancy stood like a colossus. The late J.P. Shannon, a fiddle player from Kilfarboy (a couple of miles to the north of Miltown) moved into Miltown around 1950. As a result of a childhood illness, J.P. was confined to a wheelchair and rarely ventured away from the town. Willie Clancy was to visit J.P. many times, and J.P. described him as 'the best concert flute player I ever heard . . . a natural musician'.[44]

Although remembered as a rather shy, retiring person, Willie was the focus for most of Miltown's musical activities. Perhaps part of the reason for his stature and influence was the growing interest in Ireland's only truly native instrument: the *uilleann* pipes.

Notes to Chapter 1

1   See Brian Ó Dalaigh, ed., *The Stranger's Gaze – Travels in County Clare* 1534–1950 (Ennis: Clasp Press, 1998).

2   Cf. Patrick Taylor, *The West Clare Railway* (Brighton: Plateway Press, 1994).

3   For a comprehensive survey of internal communications in the early 1930s, see Conrad M. Arensburg and Solon T. Kimball, *Family and Community in Ireland*, 3rd ed. (Ennis: Clasp Press 2001), pp. 273f. It should be noted that, excepting the closure of West Clare Railway, the basic structure of internal communications has changed little since that time.

4   Pat Flynn, 'The Inmates of Public Institutions on the Night of 30th March 1851', *Dal gCais*, vol. 11 (1993), p. 127.

5   Figures from the 2002 Census.

6   Hugh Brody, *Inishkillane: Change and Decline in the West of Ireland* (London: Jill Norman & Hobhouse, 1973), p. 51 (also contains a comprehensive bibliography of the subject).

7   The financial ties between Irish farmers and their British landlords were not finally resolved until 1938.

8   Seosamh Mac Mathúna, *Kilfarboy – A History of a West Clare Parish* (Miltown Malbay: published by the author, n.d.). Much of the historical information in this account was gleaned from this excellent publication.

9   'Clachan community: a formless cluster of small farm houses . . . lacking such village attributes as church and public house, it comprised the homes of a constantly changing number of related families.' See E. Estyn Evans, *The Personality of Ireland* (Dublin: Lilliput Press, 1992).

10   For more on this subject, see Breandán Breathnach, 'The Church and Dancing in Ireland', *Dal gCais*, vol. 6 (1982), pp. 59–71. For details of court cases concerning country house dances in County Clare, see Helen Brennan, *The Story of Irish Dance* (Dingle: Brandon, 1999), pp. 126–31.

11   Barry Taylor, 'Junior Crehan of Ballymackea Beg', *Musical Traditions*, vol. 10 (1992), pp. 30–31.

12   Tom Munnelly, *Béaloideas – the Journal of the Folklore of Ireland Society*, vol. 66 (1998), pp. 143–57. N.b.: Gatach was a malevolent magician who could change into various forms, including that of a cat. He is finally slain in this shape at a stream near Cloonlaheen, Mullagh, County Clare, in battle with Diarmuid.

13   Seamus Mac Mathúna, 'Garrett Barry', *Treoir*, series 2, no. 7 (1980), p. 4. Thanks to Thomas Johnson for pointing out this reference.

14   Harry Hughes and Muiris Ó Rócháin, eds, 'Willie Clancy: The Man and His Music', *Dal gCais*, vol. 1 (1972), p. 113.

15   See Micheál Ó Lochlainn, 'The Pipe Makers', *Dal gCais*, vol. 2 (1973), pp. 60f.

16   Seamus Mac Mathúna, 'Willie Clancy – His Life and His Music', *Dal gCais*, vol. 2 (1975), p. 79.

17   Pat Mitchell, *The Dance Music of Willie Clancy* (Dublin and Cork: Mercier, 1976), p. 9.

18   See Tom Munnelly, *Béaloideas*, vol. 66.

19   Hugh McCurtin, Jr, 'The Piper Hugh McCurtin', *Dal gCais*, vol. 6 (1982), p. 51.

20   For further information on Martin Rochford, see Harry Hughes and Muiris Ó Rócháin, 'Talking with Martin Rochford', *Dal gCais*, vol. 4 (1978), pp. 112f.

21   Terence Brown, *Ireland: A Social and Cultural History, 1922–1979* (London: Fontana, 1981), pp. 211f.

22   Fintan O'Toole, *The Irish Times Book of the Century* (Dublin: Gill & Macmillan, 1999), p. 199.

23   Junior Crehan, 'Junior Crehan Remembers', *Dal gCais*, vol. 3 (1977), p. 75.

24   See Seamus Mac Mathúna, 'Willie Clancy', p. 78.

25   Pat Mitchell, 'Willie Clancy – Some Reflections on His Life and Music', *Dal gCais*, vol. 9 (1988), p. 84. See also the introduction to Pat Mitchell, *The Dance Music of Willie Clancy*.

26   For a fuller exposition of the role of *céilí* bands, see the following: Barry Taylor, 'The Tulla Céilí Band', *Dal gCais*, vol. 9 (1988), pp. 51f; Sean McNamara, "The Liverpool Céilí Band', *Dal gCais*, vol. 9 (1988), pp. 91f; Jimmy Ward, 'The Musical Heritage of Kilfenora', *Dal gCais*, vol. 4 (1978), pp. 71f; and Barry Taylor, 'The Irish Céilí Band – a Break with Tradition?', *Dal gCais*, vol. 7 (1984), pp. 67f.

27   Willie Clancy, Michael Gorman and Margaret Barry, *Irish Pipe and Fiddle Tunes*, Top 89 (London: Topic Record Co., 1963).

28   The Laichtín Naofa Céilí Band, *An Irish Dance Party*; Harp 8 (Monaghan: Shamrock Record Co., re-issue of original recording make for the Dublin Record Co., 1959–60).

29 Seamus Mac Mathúna, 'Willie Clancy – His Life and His Music', *Dal gCais*, vol. 2 (1975), p. 80.
30 See Junior Crehan, 'Junior Crehan Remembers', p. 72.
31 Harry Hughes and Tom Munnelly, 'Marty O'Malley – The Spirit of the Country House', *Dal gCais*, vol. 7 (1984), pp. 85f.
32 The relationship between Séamus Ennis and Miltown Malbay is covered in detail in *The Séamus Ennis Story: Miltown Malbay Remembers*, Cassette MC 115 (Dublin: RTÉ, 1988), part 3.
33 Information from Tom Munnelly, *Béaloideas*.
34 Recorded conversation between Brid O'Donohue (O'Brien) and Barry Taylor, Glandine, County Clare, 2 January 2001.
35 Patrick Weston Joyce, *English as We Speak It in Ireland*; quoted in Marie McCarthy, *Passing It On* (Cork: Cork University Press, 1999), p. 61.
36 Brid O'Donohue (O'Brien) to Barry Taylor.
37 Published as Breandán Breathnach, *Folkmusic and Dances of Ireland* (Dublin: Talbot Press, 1971).
38 See Helen Brennan, *The Story of Irish Dance*, p. 10.
39 Recorded conversation between Finbar Boyle and Barry Taylor, Dublin, 23 April 1998.
40 For more information, see Steve MacDonagh, *Green and Gold: The Wrenboys of Dingle* (Dingle: Brandon, 1983).
41 Recorded conversation between Muiris Ó Rócháin and Barry Taylor, Miltown Malbay, County Clare, 25 May 1998. (Ó Rócháin's collection is now deposited in the Folklore Department at UCD.)
42 Recorded conversation between Harry Hughes and Barry Taylor, Mullagh, County Clare, 1 June 1998.
43 Muiris Ó Rócháin to Barry Taylor.
44 Barry Taylor, 'The Fiddler from Kilfarboy', *Dal gCais*, vol 8 (1986), p. 49.

Tuesday

BEFORE 10 O'CLOCK, a hundred or so dancers are assembled in Miltown's Community Hall, and Terry Moylan of Brook's Academy launches into a set that had been started on the previous day. This set is known as the Limerick tumbler and was devised by Terry. The polkas and slides that accompany the Limerick tumbler impart a particularly lively swing to proceedings, and within half an hour, the remaining figures have been completed and the dancers have added another dance to their repertoire.

After a short break, the microphone passes to Mary Friel: 'Now, the Brook's Academy staff will demonstrate the Paris set.' Terry Moylan takes time out from his teaching duties to explain that the set was collected from Dan Furey and James Keane of Labasheeda, County Clare. 'They were fairly bashful at having a dance with such an imposing title as the Paris set and for years referred to it simply as the Loughayle set. Eventually, they admitted that, in fact, it was the Paris set.'

This is a particularly graceful and intricate dance with seven figures danced in reel time. After the first figure, Mary Friel announces that in the next and future figures, all the 'gents' and those ladies dancing as gents – as seems usual in contemporary dance classes, there is a preponderance of ladies – will move on to the next set. With eleven sets packed tightly into the hall, confusion seems guaranteed, but things quickly sort themselves out and the teaching continues.

Replacing an absent gent with a lady can lead to problems. In a later figure, the gent has to detach himself from his partner following a dance 'around the house' and, whilst manoeuvring swiftly backwards, engage with his next lady. Unfortunately, a combination of the backward manoeuvre and the preponderance of ladies is causing some confusion. Resourcefully, Mary

Set dance class, Community Hall, 1999.

Friel suggests a solution. 'If you add a sixth step to the round the house, this will leave the gents facing their next partner and should help to clear up any confusion.'

* * *

A few hundred yards up the Ballard road in the Mill Theatre, Mick Mulkerrins is passing on the intricacies of Connemara *sean-nós* step dancing. This is a complicated affair involving numerous sequences of complex steps, and the dancers are required to memorise the sequences before any attempt is made at individual interpretation.

Mick explains that many of the sequences have been devised by individual dancers and demonstrates sequences devised by Joe O'Donovan of County Cork and Willie Keane of nearby Doonbeg – described by Mick as 'perhaps the finest dancer I have ever seen'. Midway through morning, the heavens open as a storm hits Miltown, causing the organisers to close the theatre's roller shutter door. Seemingly oblivious of the din outside, the dancers batter on.

Mairéad Casey demonstrating sean-nós *steps, accompanied by Mick Mulkerrins on the box, Mill Theatre*, 2000.

With more than two dozen classes taking place in St Joseph's Secondary School, you are never too far away from the sound of the fiddle, but in one quiet corner, Brian Mullins from Derry and Ian Lee from Dublin take students through the intricacies of traditional singing in both Irish and English. Brian explains that, within Ireland, the province of Ulster has a particularly strong tradition of song. 'Ulster was the last stronghold of the old Gaelic Ireland until the end of sixteenth century. Since then, it has come under the influence of both England and Scotland, giving it a very rich cultural mix.'

Brian's presentation is a highly personalised exploration of Ireland's complex English-language singing tradition. 'Although I come from a singing family, most of our songs were not what would be nowadays called traditional. They were more likely to be Victorian parlour ballads or light

Brian Mullins singing in Gleeson's of Coore, a few miles outside Miltown Malbay, 1998.

opera. Like many others of my generation, my first exposure to traditional songs came from listening to the radio in the early 1960s when the Clancy Brothers hit the big time. I also went through a period singing pop songs before really becoming involved in traditional music while at university in Bangor, Wales.

'After returning to Ireland, I was fortunate to meet many fine singers, including Len Graham and Joe Holmes from County Antrim and Eddie Butcher from Magilligan in County Derry. Eddie was an extraordinary character and absolutely mad about singing. When I first visited his house, he asked me to sing a song before I had even taken my coat off!

'Nowadays I sing mainly traditional songs, but I still occasionally like to sing the songs that I remember from my schooldays.'

The class is transfixed as Brian demonstrates his ability to handle a complicated traditional ballad and then switches to a sixties pop song.

As lunchtime approaches, Ian announces that tomorrow they will look at the treatment of love and sex in Irish-language songs. 'If you have any friends who might be interested in this topic, bring them along – everyone is welcome.' It promises to be a fascinating morning.

Chapter 2

Filling the Gap

ALONG WITH SO much of traditional music and dance, the *uilleann* pipes had suffered a great deal of neglect between the 1920s and 1940s. As a result, by the 1950s, practising pipers in Ireland were few and far between, although, perhaps, they had never been numerous.

Until the later years of the nineteenth century, the pipes were handmade by craftsmen and were the expensive tools of the professional musician. Towards the end of that century, cheap factory-made instruments such as fiddles, whistles, melodians and, of course, concertinas began to circulate in rural Ireland. The concertina provided a substitute for the pipes. Perhaps less subtle than the pipes, they were cheap and readily available, relatively simple to maintain and, at least for basic dance purposes, much simpler to play than the pipes – or even the fiddle or flute.

The founding of *Comhaltas Ceoltóirí Éireann* certainly helped to re-ignite interest in piping. In Miltown Malbay, shortly after a CCÉ branch was launched in 1955, two sets of practice pipes were purchased, one of which was loaned to J.C. Talty, leading to his winning the all-Ireland intermediate championship in 1960.

Although the early activities of CCÉ reactivated the dormant interest of many traditional musicians and their followers, as the enthusiasm of the early years began to wane in the early sixties, doubts began to surface about CCÉ's direction and policies. One of the most able and vocal critics of CCÉ was Breandán Breathnach, a piper and a keen student of Irish traditional culture, who was later to take a prominent role in the development of the School. As his disillusionment with CCÉ grew, he waged an unremitting attack on the organisation through his journal, *Ceol* (launched in 1963) – particularly with regards to its attitude to piping. Breathnach was not alone in his views: although relatively few in numbers, pipers had been prominent in the early days of the organisation, and many felt that the ever-increasing emphasis on competition, with its tendency towards standardisation of playing techniques, was now contributing to the decline of piping.

And so, following a get-together of pipers at Bettystown, County Meath, on 6 and 7 April 1968, the decision was taken to launch a pipers' organisation, which became known as Na Píobairí Uilleann (NPU). Ironically, the Bettystown gathering was actually sponsored by CCÉ and organised by its music officer (*oifigeach cheoil*), Séamus Mac Mathúna. However, at a meeting held in Dublin on 26 October, CCÉ president Labhrás Ó Murchú (now a senator) urged pipers to disband NPU and work as individuals in their local branches of CCÉ. That the meeting unanimously rejected this proposal indicates the strength of feeling of the delegates, although, in a vain last effort to preserve links, the pipers invited CCÉ to send a representative (who should be a piper) to future meetings.[1]

NPU's aim of promoting the construction and playing of the *uilleann* pipes soon began to attract the support of a number of younger pipers, many of whom were inspired by the music and personality of Willie Clancy, and visits to Miltown became a regular feature in their itinerary. NPU's newsletter, *An Píobaire*, reported one organised visit:

> In December last, a group of members spent a week [ending on 10 December 1972] in Miltown Malbay with Willie Clancy. . . [For] most of the group who knew Willie only through tape and record, the visit was

Members of the newly formed Na Píobairí Uilleann, *Bettystown, County Meath, 30 March 1968. Willie Clancy is front row, far left (photo:* Na Píobairí Uilleann).

an initiation and revealing what was embodied in the tradition. In his own quiet way, Willie realised he was the sole inheritor of Garret Barry's music, the remaining link with a treasure of the music of Clare that so exalted George Petrie one hundred and forty years ago. Willie's sense of belonging and continuity and his own generous nature multiplied that fifty-fold.[2]

Tragically, this was probably the last opportunity to enjoy the company of the great Clare piper: over the Christmas period, Willie Clancy suffered a heart attack and was taken to Galway Hospital, where he died on 24 January 1973. Although he had mentioned an illness to close friends during the previous year, his death came as a mighty blow to the people of Miltown and the wider community of musicians, dancers and singers that had flocked to his door. Willie's death is vivid in Brid O'Donohue's memory:

> I remember coming down the road from school, and one of lads came up to tell us that Willie Clancy had died. That was a big shock. I wasn't at his funeral because I wouldn't be let go off school —it's the adults that would go. . . I remember being inside at J.C.'s. I remember him crying into a towel, he was that upset. Every person was shocked that he had died because they were all such good friends, as well as the music side of it all.[3]

The *Clare Champion* reported the news:

> Times come when we are carried back through our progressions and developments, divested of our sophistication and big words to be left sprawling on our roots. Such a time was Friday, January 26 – the day the piper Willie Clancy was buried. Willie had the art of reverting us to our roots. The man was his music and his music came to us through generations of our piping and singing ancestry.[4]

Willie's standing in Miltown was such that a local committee was set up to seek a suitable way to commemorate his life. A subscription list for a memorial was advertised in the *Clare Champion*, and Harry Hughes found himself in charge of the fund: 'There was a list of names . . . They were giving the odd fiver – most people'd say a pound or whatever it'd be, a fiver – to fund whatever was going to come, but even at that point, February to Easter 1973, there was no clear idea. People were talking in terms of a statue, and so on and so forth, as a memorial. . .'[5]

To many, a commemorative statue seemed an inappropriate way to celebrate the life of a man who had revelled in the dynamic process of making music and passing on the traditions of his native Clare. Then, by a combination of circumstances, the idea of a summer school for musicians slowly began to gel.

* * *

A major beneficiary of the general upsurge of interest in Ireland's traditional music in the early 1950s had been the *céilí* bands, whose playing membership and popular support was drawn largely from the rural communities.

However, in 1962, Seán Ó Riada, Dublin-based classical musician and former music director of the Abbey Theatre, delivered a series of radio programmes in which he attempted to analyse the structure and development of Ireland's musical traditions.[6] In the series, Ó Riada mounted an attack on *céilí* bands, stating that they were '. . . badly on the wrong track and, if something is not done, may do great harm to Irish music generally'.[7]

Ó Riada proposed the formation of a 'new' type of instrumental ensemble – his 'ideal *céilí* band' – to counter the ill effects of the *céilí* band movement. In fact, this idea had already manifested itself in his ensemble *Ceoltóirí Chualann*, which came to general public notice in 1961. Unlike the *céilí* bands, whose format was largely based on the popular dance bands of the early to mid-twentieth century, *Ceoltóirí Chualann* closely resembled a chamber orchestra. Although their repertoire largely consisted of traditional dance music – and showed more than a hint of the *céilí* band origin of many of its members – its format and personnel (a mixture of traditional and classically trained musicians) also allowed other types of music to be performed. Notably, that included the work of the late seventeenth century piper, Turlough Carolan, whose music was to become increasingly popular.[8] *Ceoltóirí Chualann* also featured songs in their repertoire, utilising the talents of Cork's Seán Ó Sé and the great Connemara *sean-nós* singer Darach Ó Catháin. Although *Ceoltóirí Chualann* was relatively short-lived, its members formed the basis for the most influential and long-lasting of the new ensembles of the sixties, the Chieftains.

Ceoltóirí Chualann and the Chieftains were portents of a trend that was becoming increasingly evident – the gradual shift of traditional music from the country to the town. Although participation and interest in traditional music had not been previously restricted to the countryside, rural Ireland was, undoubtedly, its stronghold . However, in the second half of the twentieth century, it began to attract a following from large numbers of urban working class youth.

The sixties and seventies were periods of significant economic growth and social change in Ireland. P.J. Curtis commented: 'For the first time in several hundred years, a generation of young Irish men and women did not have to consider emigration as their only option. A dynamic new energy found release in this, seemingly, new Ireland, growing in confidence almost daily. That confidence permeated not only the business sector but also the arts in all forms.'[9]

Some have claimed that the prime cause for the rise in interest in traditional music in Ireland was the US folk boom of the late forties and fifties. However, probably the most potent catalyst for change was the British 'folk music revival' of the early sixties, which had taken traditional song as its focus and, along the way, drawn in many young Irish immigrants. Among those attracted to this movement – and perhaps, ultimately, the most influential in Ireland – was Luke Kelly, later to become a member of the 'ballad group' the Dubliners. Formed in 1962, the Dubliners might be said to epitomise the spirit of the ballad boom of the sixties, and their inclusive, racy and largely optimistic 'come-all-ye' style found a ready audience with the young urban population.

The ballad movement spread like wildfire, and there were few areas of Ireland that escaped its influence. In 1972, Christy Moore – another of the most influential figures in Irish music from the sixties to the present day – joined forces with Donal Lunny, Andy Irvine and piper Liam Óg Ó Floinn to form a new ensemble known as Planxty. The group was the first of the hybrid bands, which placed equal emphasis on dance music and song. Following the break-up of Planxty in 1975, the individual band members were to play increasingly influential roles in the growing Irish folk music industry. According to Mícheál Ó Súilleabháin:

> The arrival of groups such as the Chieftains and Planxty – later to have a more viable successor in the Bothy Band – opened the music to an even younger audience. This new group involvement is the single greatest factor in the present international interest in Irish traditional music. It is because of this that musicians like Micho Russell can now sit alone on a stage in Germany and receive tumultuous applause for playing the tin whistle in his own pure style.[10]

The ballad groups and instrumental ensembles such as the Chieftains represented two separate but related strands. Whereas the members of the ballad groups tended to be mainly young and urban, the members of instrumental groups were often made up of older rural musicians, some of whom had spent the forties and fifties playing in *céilí* bands.

The ballad boom was mainly centred on Dublin (but also involved Galway, Cork, Limerick and Belfast) and featured the founding of a number of British-style folk clubs, including the influential Tradition Club, based in Slattery's Bar, Capel Street, Dublin. The sixties also saw a flowering of a number of other activities, many of which were initiated by Breandán Breathnach. In addition to NPU and the magazine *Ceol*, Breathnach was also one of the major proponents for *Cumann Cheol Tíre Éireann* (the Folk Music Society of Ireland), which was established in 1971 and was to provide an academic focus for traditional music studies over the next decade.

The period has sometimes been referred to as 'the revival', which suggests that traditional music in Ireland was in its death throes. However, although certainly at a low ebb entering the second half of the twentieth century, it was still a vital part of the lives of many people, particularly those in the western counties.

Reviewing the sudden growth of interest in Irish music among the young, Terence Brown commented: 'It must be stressed, however, that this development was simply an aspect of the more general social changes that were in progress in the period. The demographic, economic and educational changes . . . had created a new social group with the leisure and freedom from responsibility to follow interests and inclinations.'[11]

Liam Ó Floinn (left) and Willie Clancy, early1970s (photo: Mal Whyte).

Having been fed on a diet of imported and often poorly adapted pop culture for much of the twentieth century, some young people embarked on the search for a culture that might more accurately reflect their roots, and many found that traditional music, song and dance was still alive and well in areas such as west Clare. This led many to the discovery that the culture of the *clachan* embodied concepts of community and sharing that were more in keeping with their views than the crass commerciality of life in the late twentieth century, giving rise to the informal cultural tourism of the late sixties and early seventies which was to provide the inspiration for the School.

* * *

Following the death of Willie Clancy, an idea that had been rumbling away in the back of Muiris Ó Rócháin's mind now came to the fore. Ó Rócháin's concept was to blend elements from established Irish summer schools, such as the Yeats and Merriman, with elements from the long-established Scandinavian summer schools for traditional culture. However, Ó Rócháin felt that the often dry, academic approach found at such events would be unlikely to have much appeal to the young people now coming into traditional music. His idea was to make the musicians the focus of a school of traditional music and to expose as many people – especially young people – as possible to their influence.

In the early 1970s, Ireland was awash with traditional music of all kinds. With folk clubs and folk festivals burgeoning throughout the country, and, west Clare having become a Mecca for young enthusiasts, a major musical festival in Miltown Malbay might, in retrospect, have seemed an inevitable form of tribute. However, Ó Rócháin was determined to avoid an exploitative event. Although in the early stages he had not evolved a defined structure for his concept, a model was provided for Ó Rócháin by the activities of Willie Clancy: 'Even in discussion before Willie died, it was Willie [that] was the ideal man. He knew so much about the music that you'd literally expose kids to him; his charisma, his mastery of the pipes, his singing and the whistle, the slow airs, he had all this. He was the ideal man. So what we tried to do was follow on from that.'[12]

Other than commercial promoters, the only organisation with the experience needed to mount a major traditional music event at that time was CCÉ. In fact, most of the people involved in Irish music in Miltown in the 1960s and seventies were members of CCÉ, and many had already been involved in organising events such the Clare county *fleadh*.

At the CCÉ annual convention in the summer of 1972, interest had already been expressed in the establishment of a summer school for traditional musicians. So, at a function in Ennis held in November 1972, Ó Rócháin (a CCÉ member) took the opportunity to discuss locating such a school in Miltown with CCÉ president Labhrás Ó Murchú. Ironically, the concept might have been forgotten, but Willie's death brought the idea back into Muiris Ó Rócháin's mind.

At a meeting of the memorial committee in the house of musician and singer Paddy Joe McMahon (now Haugh's butcher shop in Miltown), Ó Rócháin related his earlier informal discussion with Ó Murchú and proposed the organisation of a summer school. Paddy Joe McMahon, who had been a key figure in the launch of the Miltown branch of CCÉ back in 1955, was highly supportive, and the proposal was quickly accepted, with Ó Rócháin instructed to contact CCÉ headquarters in Dublin to get things started. CCÉ instructed Séamus Mac Mathúna to liase with the local committee, a task that was, ultimately, to provide him with many difficulties.

By 1973, the world of Irish music, and particularly the world of pipers, had changed significantly. Under the leadership of Breandán Breathnach and with the active and committed support of Willie Clancy, NPU had largely replaced CCÉ as the focal point for piping.

Although the Willie Clancy Summer School was conceived as an event for all traditional musicians, Willie's dedication to the pipes and his involvement in the founding and development of NPU necessitated a leading role for both the instrument and the organisation. Moreover, Willie's untimely death had left pipers with a deep sense of loss, and the members of NPU were eager to participate in any activity to commemorate his contribution to the piping tradition. Thus, when Ó Rócháin (for the local committee) and Séamus Mac Mathúna (for CCÉ) sat down to plan the first school, the active involvement of NPU, or at least its members, was taken for granted.

As a close friend and long-time musical colleague of Willie Clancy and in recognition of his scholarship, Breandán Breathnach was invited and agreed to give an opening lecture on Willie. For CCÉ, there were problems as to whether Breathnach's title of chairman of NPU could appear in the School's publicity material, as, effectively, *they* did not even recognise the existence of NPU. On the other hand, Breathnach was reluctant to share a platform with representatives of an organisation which, in his opinion, had contributed little to piping and had endeavoured to scupper the pipers' organisation. For a while there was deadlock, and by June 1973 correspondence was flying backwards and forwards between CCÉ headquarters and Miltown.

With much of the organisation for the School already in hand, a compromise was sought, and Séamus Mac Mathúna, a good friend of Willie Clancy, a fine musician in his own right and a native of west Clare, agreed to give the opening lecture. Séamus de Brún, as president of CCÉ, would deliver an opening speech. Although all parties were placated for the time being, the situation was far from satisfactory; and in July 1973, Ó Rócháin was summoned to meet the executive of CCÉ in Dublin:

> I contacted Sean Reid, and I told Sean to contact Peter O'Loughlin, Martin Talty – there were only four or five of us anyway… We met with the executive of CCÉ. We weren't too happy with what was happening, and we were quite willing to pull out, but I think that they had gone a step too far with the publicity and everything else. There was an agreement that we would row in this year and we would be involved, but we just wanted them to know that we felt that the pipers shouldn't have been sidelined because, after all, Willie Clancy was a piper.[13]

Not surprisingly, NPU were less than happy at the turn of events: 'It has transpired that responsibility for running this festival [the School] has been handed over to *Comhaltas Ceoltóirí Éireann* and that body has issued directions that no mention of NPU may be made in publicity issued about the event. Members are to regard this as a release from any further co-operation which they may have made individually.'[14]

* * *

With the opening day scheduled for 28 July, there was no time to be lost in finalising plans. It is a tribute to Ó Rócháin's and Mac Mathúna that the programme devised so quickly in 1973 has stood the test of time. For Ó Rócháin the issues were clear: the focus of the event would be on the music and its performers, who would be accessible to the largest numbers of people. He had observed the increasing trend within CCÉ to treat the musicians contributing to their events as something of a sideshow:

> I'll give you an example from a *fleadh* . . . there was a great Connemara singer, Johnny Mháirtín Learaí Mac Donncha from Carna. I met Johnny as I passed down the *sráid* [street] – there was no one to meet him. He went up about the accommodation, down to the office. [But] all the committee . . . were running after the fellow who was opening it, this ambassador. They hadn't time to talk to this man who was a prime artist. So, I got him accommodation and things. And this bloody

ambassador, the same fellow, was withdrawn about six months after for embezzlement! But, that's the thing, their priorities. They wouldn't think of an artist as an important person.[15]

The programme was fairly straightforward: mornings would be devoted to teaching, with classes in pipe playing and making, whistle and flute playing, fiddle playing and *sean-nós* singing. Each afternoon, there was to be a recital in the parochial hall, and in the evening a formal lecture would be presented on some aspect of traditional or local culture (not confined solely to music and dance). Some additional lectures were to be presented during the morning programme, presumably to cater for those not attending music classes.

In addition to the classes, recitals and lectures, several key events have remained a feature in all subsequent years, including opening the School on a Saturday evening with a major lecture, the first having been Mac Mathúna's 'Willie Clancy – the Man and His Music'.[16] As testimony to his work on behalf of the School, in 1985, following his death, the opening lecture was dedicated to Breandán Breathnach. Another long-standing tradition has been a mass held in Irish at the local Catholic church, followed by a visit to Willie Clancy's grave, with an oration, a piped lament and wreath laying. Finally, events close on the following Saturday night with a concert, which largely features the musicians who have contributed to the week's teaching programme and recitals.

For many years, Sunday night was the occasion of a *céilí* featuring east Clare's Tulla Céilí Band. This *céilí* has been replaced by a complete programme of dance activities, featuring a number of today's leading *céilí* bands, including the Kilfenora, Michael Sexton, Esker Riada, Abbey, Matt Cunningham, Four Courts, Tulla, Four Star, Glenside, Templehouse, Emerald, Swallows Tail, Turloughmore and Shaskeen. Not surprisingly, those with the Tulla Céilí Band are the most popular.

Piping activity in that first school was somewhat limited. Whilst the decision to open the School with Mac Mathúna's oration on the life of Willie Clancy may have guaranteed the involvement of CCÉ and probably saved the event from financial disaster, the withdrawal of NPU from official participation left a sizeable hole in the programme, which was only partially filled by inviting a number of pipers on an individual basis. These included Sean Reid, Peadar O'Loughlin, the two Lavin Brothers from County Roscommon and Séamus Ennis. However, the dissatisfaction expressed to the organisers by the piping students over the piping workshops clearly demonstrated that, if the School was to gain credibility among pipers, the cooperation and involvement of NPU was essential.

Fortunately, due to the network of contacts that Ó Rócháin and Mac Mathúna had established and the cooperation of the local musical fraternity (which was well represented on the local committee), there were few problems with the other instruments. The programme for the first year, which looks like a *Who's Who* of resident Clare musicians, included Martin Talty, Sean Reid, Peadar O'Loughlin, Paddy Murphy, Junior Crehan and singer Tom Lenihan. They were joined by Bobby Casey, who made the return trip from London, and Dublin-based but west Clare-born fiddle and concertina player John Kelly.

Although CCÉ had agreed to underwrite the costs of the School, finances were still tight, even with the cash raised by the local appeal. From Dublin, the Tradition Club stepped in. Organisers Tom Crehan, Finbar Boyle, Kevin Conneff and Sean Corcoran suggested holding fund-raising concerts in Dublin.

Evening céilí with the Tulla Céilí Band, 2000.

As Finbar Boyle recalls:

Somebody approached us in the Tradition Club to raise some funds for [the School], and we ran a couple of concerts – one big concert, I think, in Liberty Hall. We filled Liberty Hall with whatever musicians were around in Dublin at the time. A crowd of them came up from Clare as well, and whatever was left over after the administration expenses was put to the organisation of the School. That went on for a couple of years then. It seemed that there was a Willie Clancy concert every year in Dublin for about three years, four years maybe, and we raised quite a lot of money.[17]

All the main organisers of the Tradition Club were either from Dublin or small-town Ireland, and all had come to traditional music during the renewal of interest in traditional music in the 1960s and 1970s.

For the young Brid O'Donohue, that first summer school was a revelation:

It was my first year in secondary school, and that year I remembered having a summer job working as a waitress in Daly's in Kilmurry. I

Open air concert, Miltown Malbay, 1975. Left to right: Michael Falsey, Bobby Casey, Junior Crehan, Seán Reid, Andy Conroy, Pat Mitchell, James Kelly (hidden) and John Kelly, Sr (photo: Liam McNulty).

remember going in on the Wednesday or the Thursday – it was big thing, I was only thirteen at the time. I met Muiris and he said, 'Come on up and I'll show you what's going on.' That would have been the first year with the classes up at the Tech, and I remember going in and getting a whistle and going in to Mick Crehan, who was teaching at the time. I did nothing only by ear, and he was up on the board and saying, 'This is a cut and this is a roll. This is what you call a cut before a roll – as a roll is made up of a cut and a tap.' I knew what I was doing sounded OK, but I never heard it minced down and spoken about. So I thought that was very strange and it all made sense, but I said, 'Sure, that's what I was doing anyway.' But to hear it in words and to see all these ones from wherever they were from looking up to him and trying it and getting it![18]

At that moment, little could the thirteen-year-old Brid guess the momentous role that the School was to play in her future life.

Notes to Chapter 2

1   Breandán Breathnach, 'Na Píobairí Uilleann', *Ceol*, vol. 3, no. 3 (1969), p. 77. Whether CCÉ ever sent such a representative is not known to the author.
2   Anon., 'Willie Clancy', *An Píobaire*, no. 12 (1973), p. 8.
3   Recorded conversation between Brid O'Donohue (O'Brien) and Barry Taylor, Glandine, County Clare, 2 January 2001.
4   For full report, see Eithne Earley, 'Burial of the Piper – Willie Clancy', *The Clare Champion*, 2 February 1973.
5   Recorded conversation between Harry Hughes and Barry Taylor, Mullagh, County Clare, 1 June 1998.
6   *Our Musical Heritage* – broadcast on Radio Éireann from 7 July to 13 October 1962.
7   Thomas Kinsella and Tomás Ó Canainn, *Our Musical Heritage* (Portlaoise: Dolmen Press, 1982), p. 79.
8   See Donal O'Sullivan, *Carolan: The Life Times and Music of an Irish Harper* (London: Routledge & Keegan Paul), 1958.
9   P. J. Curtis, *Notes from the Heart* (Dublin: Torc, 1994), p. 18.
10 Quoted *ibid.*, p. 26.
11 Terence Brown, *Ireland: A Social and Cultural History: 1922–1979* (London: Fontana, 1981), pp. 276–77.
12 Recorded conversation between Muiris Ó Rócháin and Barry Taylor, Miltown Malbay, County Clare, 25 May 1998.
13 *Ibid.*
14 Document recorded in Muiris Ó Rócháin to Barry Taylor.
15 Muiris Ó Rócháin to Barry Taylor.
16 *Ibid*.
17 Recorded conversation between Finbar Boyle and Barry Taylor, Dublin, 23 April 1998.
18 Brid O'Donohue to Barry Taylor.

Wednesday

LTHOUGH THE CLASSES for most instruments are spread far and wide around Miltown, the pipers are unusual in being centralised around the Social Services Centre in the Ballard road. For the duration of the School, members of N*a Píobairí Uilleann* (NPU) staff are on hand either at the centre or in the shop in the Community Hall.

This morning, NPU's Liam McNulty has a problem: 'I've just heard that one of the tutors isn't available to take his class this morning. What a time to tell me. If I'd have known last night, we had people standing by to cover, but at this hour. . .' Liam shakes his head in exasperation and tries to work out how he can cover the gap.

Elsewhere in the centre, several pipers are starting the complex process of reed making under the watchful eye of Dave Hegarty. He explains to the group that each reed is different and must be precisely matched to the individual pipe chanter. One piper has brought back a reed made by Dave the year before: 'I've got another reed that I've been using for five years, but I need a spare one. I can't get this one going as well as the other.'

Dave sets to work on the intricate process of fettling the reed. At one stage, he shakes a small pile of bamboo dust on the workbench: 'Did you hear the story about the pipe-maker who was too mean to give you the dust of his cane?' Apparently, this is not a joking matter, as even the dust from the cut bamboo is to play an essential part in correcting the delinquent reed. Dave applies a mixture of dust and nail varnish to the errant reed – all part of the process of producing just the right sound from this complex instrument.

In a corner of the workshop, Tommy Kearney from Waterford is having some trouble with his beautiful set of Rowsome pipes. Like many of the musical instruments played by musicians attending the School, these pipes have a historic as well as a musical value. Tommy, one of the veterans of piping, retains all his skill and has a keen ear: 'I don't seem to able to get them in tune at all.' Donncha Keegan lends a hand, whilst Tommy regales listeners with stories of pipers and piping. 'That Sean Dempsey whose photo's in the latest edition of *An Píobaire*, he played before Hitler, you know. Apparently Hitler commented that he liked the sound of the *uilleann* pipes much more than the war pipes.'

Donncha is still having problems tuning the pipes to Tommy's satisfaction. 'You're hard work,' he comments. 'Couldn't you have waited until Sunday when we'll be gone?'

Thomas Johnson from Sweden asks Tommy Kearney if he can photograph the Rowsome pipes. 'You're welcome,' says Tommy.

'I've never seen them before: they are beautiful,' says Thomas, who is in the workshop to make a new reed for his Bb chanter. 'My pipes were made by Dave Williams – he works out of Grimsby in east Yorkshire. They're an excellent set, and I'm really pleased with them.'

By this time, Dave Hegarty has fitted the refurbished reed and is trying out the chanter. 'It's getting better, but it's still not quite right.' Meanwhile, under his watchful eye, the reed-making process goes on all around.

Dave Hegarty (seated centre) demonstrates reed-making techniques and tips to Peter Carbery (standing, with glasses) and other pipers, 1998.

Between times, pipers wander in and out of the workshop eager for the advice of Donncha and Dave on some aspect of pipe mechanics.

The conversation between Tommy Kearney and Thomas Johnson has turned to the pipers of earlier years, with stories about the Dorans, Tony Rainey and many, many more. 'The old pipers had to be proficient in reed making as well as piping,' comments Tommy. 'There were no workshops such as this in the old days.'

So the morning passes – a hive of industry but with always time for a tune and a story.

* * *

At the break, the teachers and their pupils gather at the centre, with the latest edition of *An Píobaire* exciting much interest and comment. A student from Argentina is found a place in Gay McKeon's class, and Liam is still anxious about the class with the missing teacher but is reassured to hear that the absentee has returned to his duties.

Donncha Keegan (centre), pipers' workshop, 2001.

Tommy Kearney in the pipers' workshop, 1993.

In the old library at St Joseph's School, Paddy Glackin and Cathal Goan are attempting the near impossible as, in a single week, 'The Scope of Irish Music' will range the entire panorama of Irish music. Although originally aimed at the up-and-coming generation of musicians, the class mainly consists of non-musicians, with a large percentage of adult and non-Irish students. The first item of the morning is a demonstration of *uilleann* piping from Pádraig Mac Mathúna, the son of legendary broadcaster Ciarán Mac Mathúna. As he straps on his pipes, Pádraig explains the historical development of the pipes and piping and surprises many of his audience: 'You know, at the end of the nineteenth century, there were probably more pipers in the USA than in Ireland.'

Observing Pádraig's routine, Paddy Glackin chips in with a story about piper Séamus Ennis: 'Séamus always made a great performance of putting

Paddy Cronin (left) and Paddy Glackin, 2002.

on the pipes. He once managed to complete a concert performance at Trinity without playing a single tune – and still left the stage to a standing ovation!'

The session ends with Pádraig and Paddy playing a selection of reels together.

After the tea break, Paddy announces that the class has a real treat coming up: the appearance of the Kerry fiddle player Paddy Cronin. Although Paddy lived for many years in the USA, he tells the class that he had learned the fiddle from the legendary Sliabh Luachra musician Pádraig O'Keeffe of Gleanntán. 'In those days, everyone had their own style of playing, but by the time the Radio Éireann mobile recording van came to the area in the 1940s and fifties, there were only about five fiddle players left.'

Paddy cut his musical teeth playing at house dances, mainly for polka sets, but comments: 'Pádraig O'Keeffe didn't like polkas too much, but he had to play them for the dancers. In the old days, players didn't have too many tunes, and if you learn from music, you can have too many – it's easy to forget tunes. I made up a good few tunes, but I can't remember most of them because I haven't written them down.'

In the final session, the theme turns to song with the introduction of Mairéad Ní Dhomhnaill. Mairéad is familiar to some of the audience through her appearances with groups such as the Bothy Band, Skara Brae and Touchstone, as well as solo performances and duets with her sister Tríona. 'I come from a singing family – my father Aodh was a singer and flute player from Rannafast, County Donegal, and collected songs for the old Folklore Commission. I learned a lot of my songs from my aunt, Neilí Ní Dhomhnaill, who sang in both Irish and English. During the 1980s, a few singers began to get together over weekends, and this gave me the opportunity to meet and learn from a whole variety of different singers.' The morning ends with Mairéad singing a selection of songs in both Irish and English and her audience clamouring for details of her recordings.

'You can buy them all in the shop,' shouts Paddy.

Chapter 3

The Challenge

THE FIRST WILLIE Clancy Summer School had been a success, with around eighty students travelling to Miltown. But when it was all over, it was time to think of the future.

The first issue facing the School's organisers was the situation regarding CCÉ and NPU – and the portents were not auspicious! In an interview with *Raidió na Gaeltachta* in the week of the first School, Ó Rócháin had commented that he thought there should be no constraints on participation because of membership of 'X or Y musical organisation'. This was simply an expression of Ó Rócháin's – and the committee's – view of the inclusive nature of the School: that it should involve all those participating in the making of Irish music. However, the interview provoked a stern response from officials of CCÉ, who claimed that the programme was biased and demanded their say. This was agreed, and a later broadcast featured a discussion between CCÉ president Séamus de Brun, Martin Talty and Sean Reid.[1]

However, in the months that followed the first school, it became increasingly obvious that CCÉ were beginning to detach themselves from proceedings. In a 1973 edition of the organisation's journal, *Treoir*, tucked away on the last page under the title 'Our Whole National Fibre Is Being Seriously Challenged', was a short statement from President de Brún. Couched in the highly charged nationalist rhetoric that had repelled many of the founders of the organisation, it stated that:

> . . . our spiritual and cultural aspirations are being attacked in a subtle and persistent manner. While it is generally admitted that our music is

making satisfactory progress, it is obvious that our native language and Irish way of life are being seriously challenged . . . This threat must be met with vigour and determination . . . Above all, there must be no retreat. All those seriously interested in the facts of our national identity – our language, music and traditions, must speak out and demand their rights. The time for silence and lip service is past. The majority of the Irish people wish to have their national identity preserved and now is the time for them to say so . . . It is sad because we are sharply reminded that the late Willie Clancy has gone to his eternal reward; it is an occasion of joy inasmuch as that the initiation of Scoil Éigse clearly demonstrates our desire to honour and perpetuate in a fitting way, the memory of not only a great musician but also a great Irishman.[2]

However, in the same issue, the 'Activity Report' for the CCÉ annual congress was painting a different vision for the future of the *Scoil Éigse*:

Our first annual Scoil Éigse was held this year in Miltown Malbay and was dedicated to the memory of the late Willie Clancy . . . This first venture was a success in many ways and Scoil Éigse '74 [Note: not Willie Clancy '74] will be further developed with a view to linking it up with the proposed cultural institute. We wish to thank the local committee in Miltown Malbay, the teachers and lecturers for their work. *The venue for Scoil Éigse '74 has not yet been decided.*[3] [My italics]

There it was in black and white. After their experiences of the first year, CCÉ had decided that enough was enough and were pulling out, leaving the local committee to sort out the future. But by now Ó Rócháin had a clear view of what was needed. If a school was to be mounted in the name of Willie Clancy, it needed the strong support of the country's pipers, and the only organisation that could deliver this was NPU. However, with the gap between NPU and CCÉ now widened to a chasm, there was no chance that the two organisations might participate together in the School in future years. However, in the first year, without the support of CCÉ and particularly Séamus Mac Mathúna, the local committee would have faced an uphill battle to mount such an ambitious enterprise.

In spite of the success of the first year, it was going to be a struggle for the committee to keep their heads above water following the withdrawal of CCÉ. As the School did not command the almost universal respect it enjoys today, it would have been easy to accept unfettered commercial sponsorship. However, as Muiris Ó Rócháin is keen to stress, one of the main reasons for its survival has been its refusal to bow to commercial pressures:

The School was never set up anything to do with economics. It's a totally cultural business. . . [T]here were times, financially, I remember having barely [enough] – fortunately, there was no one in it, no one getting paid as such. It made it very easy that we all had our own jobs to do – although we probably put in more time with the Willie Clancy School than we did with the day job. . .

I remember meeting one of the corporate managers of the Bank of Ireland in Ennis, at a *slógadh* . . . He said, 'I'll give you a thousand pound to set up a set competition.' So I said, 'I'm grateful to you, but I couldn't accept it. Competitions are totally against our philosophy. What we have is something that people come and they learn, they enjoy it and, hopefully, it rubs off. . .' He said, 'You're the first person that ever refused money from me!'[4]

In spite of being faced with a mountain of work in repeating the success of the first year, particularly without CCÉ, the imperative of honouring their friend Willie Clancy drove the organisers on. Besides the members of Dublin's Tradition Club, many sympathetic supporters around the world, the local community and, now, NPU rallied to help the School survive.

As preparations for 1974 gathered pace, *An Píobaire* announced that:

Word has been received from *Coisde Chuimhneachtain Willie Clancy* [the Willie Clancy Commemoration Committee] that a school to be dedicated almost entirely to pipes and piping is being arranged for the period 20–27 July next year at Miltown. Last year's event was marred by the machinations of musical wardhealers [*sic*] and it is reassuring to know that steps have been taken to prevent a re-occurrence of last year's debacle. Members who decide to participate in this school can confidentially look forward to a week packed with enjoyable and profitable activities. Classes in all aspects of pipe making are being planned, bag, bellows and reed making will be demonstrated and what is left of the day will be occupied by lectures, exhibitions and tutorials. Informal meetings of pipers and conviviality will doubtless borrow mornings. As this advanced notice will permit members who arrange their holidays to fit in with the School, it is expected that this commemorative event will vie with the annual *Tionól*.[5]

Although there is an emphasis in this statement on the piping aspects of the School, in fact the programme for 1974 was nearly identical to that of the previous year, thus confirming that most of those involved in its organisation envisaged the School as an event to celebrate the widest aspects of

Irish music. However, because piping activities take up a lot of space and because of the heritage of Willie Clancy, piping will always be to the fore at the School. Even so, in terms of sheer numbers of participants, pipers have been considerably outnumbered by both players of other instruments and latterly set dancers.[6]

Although finances were tight, the 1974 School proved successful, with student numbers slightly increased from the initial year. So, following the first two successful years and now confident of the support of the overwhelming majority of Ireland's traditional music community, the organising committee decided to change the date of the School from the beginning of August to early July.

From the foundation of CCÉ in 1951, its flagship event had been the annual *Fleadh Cheoil na hÉireann*, held for many years on the August Bank Holiday weekend (in Ireland, the first complete weekend in August). Initially, the event had been largely attended by musicians, and its activities had focused on the programme of competitions, concerts and musical demonstrations. However, as the event grew in popularity through the fifties, it spilled out from the halls into neighbouring pubs, and, gradually, the informal sessions began to dominate events, attracting large crowds of casual visitors. In 1963, the *fleadh* had been held in Mullingar, and the close proximity to Dublin combined with the holiday weekend had resulted in a massive attendance. On the days following the event, Irish papers were full of accounts of drunken and violent behaviour, which seemed to threaten the whole existence of CCÉ. As a result, the date of the *fleadh* was changed to a non-holiday weekend (the last weekend in August) and held in locations increasingly remote from Dublin, such as Bundoran, County Donegal, and Listowel, County Kerry.

At first, the Willie Clancy Summer School had been held close to the August Bank Holiday weekend, but having having seen the problems with the *fleadh*, the School's organising committee decided that a change was due.

A measure of financial security was provided by the decision of the Arts Council to make an annual grant to the School from 1975, and its finances were further underpinned when Clare County Council contributed an annual grant in 1976.

By 1976, the School had become a significant feature of the musical life of Ireland, and word was spreading even further afield, as this editorial in *An Píobaire* suggests:

Scoil Éigse Willie Clancy 1976 (3–10 July) was in many respects the most successful to date. The pipers' workshop conducted by Dan

O'Dowd, with Johnny Burke, Michael Joe Sexton, Eugene Lambe and Tom White, presented a scene of bustle and activity from morning to night, with twenty and more members working like beavers at making reeds, bags and bellows, chanters and blow-pipes. Twenty people attended the piping classes conducted by Pat Mitchell (senior), Sean Donnelly (intermediate) and Breandán Breathnach (beginners). Dublin, Derry and Belfast, Paris, Rotterdam, Antwerp and Liverpool were among the cities represented.[7]

But there was also a downside to the growth of the School. Miltown is a small town and in the early days lacked the facilities to cope with an ever-increasing influx of visitors. In fact, the lack of facilities was something that was to plague the School to more recent times. Back in 1976, complaints centred on overcrowded accommodation and shortcomings in the standard of the toilets in some of the town's public buildings. The editor of An Píobaire was also concerned with increases to school fees, though it must be said that these have always been extremely modest. Even by 2002, fees had only reached €90 (UK£65), a figure that includes around eighteen hours of tuition and admission to lectures and recitals.

Nevertheless, by 1976 the official attendance had tripled from the first year and was fast approaching 250. The time had come for a major overhaul in the organisation of the School, and this eventually led to a change in the make-up of the committee. Following a number of policy disagreements, some of the original members withdrew from the organising committee, leaving a slimmed-down body which included Muiris Ó Rócháin, Martin Talty, Junior Crehan, Paddy Joe McMahon and Sean Reid.

Perhaps as a reaction to the way that CCÉ had seemed to decline into a committee-bound bureaucracy, the School committee tended to spurn formal trappings. Until the committee was reformed into the board of a limited company in 1988, the event proceeded successfully without any written constitution or mission statement.

Unfortunately, Paddy Joe McMahon was in indifferent health for a great deal of the period following the reorganisation, and this severely curtailed his activities. Sadly, Sean Reid passed away during the Whit Weekend of 1978, leaving an effective working committee of three. At this stage, the backing of NPU and, in particular, Breandán Breathnach became even more critical.

The participation of NPU and a substantial body of the piping fraternity from 1974 meant that the School could now truly meet the aspirations of its founders. However, as Harry Hughes explained, although activities in

Miltown were fairly integrated, the pipers tended to rather keep themselves to themselves:

> Of course, they were an independent component, too, because they looked after their own area, their own section, their own school. They looked after the bookshop. They did their own registration until they handed over their registration to us. So they did all that work them-selves. They would be the one unit that would be very organised; they would come in with an administration. Some fiddle players came in as, maybe, CCÉ members, or they simply come in as fiddlers – and flute players, tin whistle players, concertina players. But these were people who had an organisation and no doubt with a mission statement behind them as well.[8]

By 1981, student enrolments had grown to over 400, and to over 600 by 1987.[9] This rapid and, to some extent, unexpected growth in student num-bers was to provide the next stepping stone for Brid O'Donohue. After her experiences of the first year, Brid was anxious to ensure that no summer job would stand in the way of her participation in the School, and she rapidly became a familiar figure in the organising team. However, her responsibili-ties didn't stop her participating in the various School activities, including attending whistle classes under Mick Crehan and Darach de Brún. Then, one morning during the third year:

> I remember that they had more whistle players than they expected, and Muiris came in and called me out, saying, 'Here, will you take that crowd?' And that was my first class. I remember that I hardly spoke a word. Then they took a survey of whether they liked the class or not, and they all liked it – and I took one every year! I was very young, say about fifteen. I was very young anyway to be doing that. I'd say it'd be the third year [1975] and I'm teaching there since . . . I suppose I picked it up from sitting in a class situation. If I hadn't sat in a formal class situation, I wouldn't have known what way to go about it. I've done the same thing ever since: I sit them around me in a semi-circle, get them all to play a tune and judge my class from that. I remember my first year in particular, everyone was pretty advanced, but I was given the weaker half, and here I was starting off with advanced fel-lows. I'd have been better off with beginners! But I always had advanced, and in a way it was easier, because you had the ones who were able to play and they wanted tunes. And I thought it was dead easy – I was able to do rolls for someone asking me to show. But I'd

say it was a good five or six years before I got into the hang of chatting to the people in between. I very rarely spoke to them, I barely said my name. Sometimes at the end of the class, someone would say, 'What's your name?' . . . I couldn't relax to talk to my people. You know, I used to take photos, because I was young and a teenager, trying to get autographs from different countries!'[10]

Nearly thirty years later, Brid would still be teaching at the School with, by this time, her own children attending as students.

It was inevitable that, as years passed, some changes would be made. For example, in response to growing demand, concertina classes were added to the programme in 1980. The concertina is an instrument that has been closely connected with County Clare, and Ó Rócháin was keen to ensure that tuition would be of the highest standard. At the time, the concertina was only just emerging to take its place alongside the fiddle, flute and pipes, and Noel Hill, from Lissycasey, was the only performer of national repute.

Noel Hill and his class, 1992. Noel's students are writing down a new tune from the sheet pinned to the blackboard.

Ó Róchain persuaded Hill to join the teaching staff, and he has remained as leader of the concertina group until this day.[11]

It was another addition to the already crowded programme that produced the most dramatic change. Muiris Ó Róchain remembers the events that led up to this:

> I was in Ennis at the *Fleadh Nua* [the national showcase event organised annually by CCÉ in Ennis], and I went to a workshop by Joe Donovan of Cork. I was very impressed with the way that Joe was able to articulate. He was a great dancer to start with, but he was able to articulate what he was doing, and he also had a great knowledge of the history of dance. I was sitting now at this very table [in Muiris' home kitchen], and someone said we should bring in set dancing . . . it was Martin [Talty]. I said, 'Look, I have a man in mind, Joe Donovan.' I went out to the phone before we finished: 'Joe, would you like to come to Miltown next year?' 'Delighted,' he said. That was how that actually happened . . . it went on from that really [until] Brook's Academy came in.[12]

The general decline in interest in the traditions of the countryside had been particularly devastating for the dance. The shift in the venue for traditional music from the private house to the public house that occurred in the 1960s may have helped ensure the survival of the music, but it did little to help the set dance. Occasionally, it was possible to find both music and dance in the pub in the sixties, as some publicans saw further potential to increase trade,[13] but, in the long term, dancing tended to die out in Clare pubs, with only Nell and Jimmy Gleeson's pub (situated in Coore, about halfway between Miltown and Mullagh) providing a vivid reminder of past times. In general, 'céilí dances' in halls and marquees mainly consisted of a mixture of 'céilí and old-time', with the 'Siege of Ennis' and the 'Bridge of Athlone' providing the alternative to waltzes, quick-steps and, later, jive. By the 1970s, set dancing – the most popular form of dance practised in the country houses (particularly in west Clare) – had virtually died out there, and many of the old dances survived only in the memories of the older generation.

Although the founding of CCÉ in 1951 had sparked some interest in dancing, the new organisation generally focused its activities on the music. Competitions run by both CCÉ and the Gaelic Athletic Association (GAA) helped maintain some level of interest in the sets, but many dancers saw the competitive element as a negative and divisive factor, that was changing the character of the various dances.

In the mid to late seventies, interest in set dancing began to rise, probably because of a realisation among the new enthusiasts that the music that was so exciting in a session or concert was actually intended for dancing rather than listening. This enabled those who did not play instruments or sing to participate in the music for the first time in several generations.[14] Perhaps nothing is more indicative of the dislocation of set dancing from dance music than its absence from the School until the tenth year (1982), by which time the growth in interest of dancing, nationally, had made its inclusion inevitable.

In that first dance class in 1982, Joe and Siobhán Donovan spent the entire week teaching one set – the Kerry set. Terry Moylan remembers it well: 'We needed the entire week! They spent a little time doing a couple of the simple *céilí* dances as well, which we hated – it wasn't what we were there for. That was the first time I met Johnny O'Leary and Julia Clifford. Joe brought them in to play for us on one of the days. Timmy McCarthy was a member of that first class, too.'[15]

Joe and Siobhán O'Donovan teaching the beginners' set dancing class, 1992.

In 1983, Joe and Siobhán Donovan were again the only act in town, and Terry recalls that their main task was to teach the Caledonian set, with a little attention paid to figure and couple dances. However, the most significant event that year was a performance of the Lancers set by dancers from Crusheen at the concert, following which arrangements were made for Terry and his friends to visit Crusheen later in the year.

Fired with enthusiasm, they returned to Dublin intent on setting up some kind of organisation to facilitate the learning of sets. Buoyed up with an offer of space at the premises of NPU, a club-cum-class was started in the autumn of 1982, and thus Brook's Academy was launched.[16] Throughout its life, the Academy has been closely allied to the NPU: it activities were first held at the premises of NPU, its collection of dances was published by NPU (with an introduction by Breandán Breathnach), and a good many of its initial members were also members of NPU. It is not surprising that Brook's Academy should also become closely tied to the School.

Sadly Martin Talty was not to see the results of the introduction of set dancing. His passing in 1982 brought an era to an end and proved a big loss to the School. While Ó Rócháin and Hughes have been the driving force behind the School, the older generation of musicians, such as Junior Crehan and Martin Talty, were the link into the rich traditional culture of the area. As a lifelong friend of Willie Clancy, an excellent whistle player and piper, a founder member of both CCÉ and NPU, and a one-time member of both the Tulla and Laichtín Naofa Céilí Bands, Talty's traditional pedigree was impeccable. Harry Hughes, who had been befriended by Talty on his arrival in Miltown, saluted his unique qualities:

> Martin was a very sociable individual . . . Now, Willie Clancy would have been very shy – well, in other words, you take a little time to know [him]. But Martin was there always and ready with anecdotes and stories and embellishment and everything else on the personalities. . . . Talty, in a way, was a kind of mentor to me in my re-introduction to traditional music. I'm not saying that every story that Talty told me was perfect in all details, but I would say that there was a basic structure of the story which was true, and Talty, in his own inimitable way, would colour a story and embellish it – and it was all the better for that! The man was remarkably gifted to tell a good story.[17]

For visitors to the School from 1973 to 1982, Martin Talty seemed to be an ever-present figure, introducing recitals and lectures, organising and conducting classes, and playing tunes on the whistle in late night sessions in pubs. As Hughes said, 'He was a presiding figure, always on the fringes and presiding.'[18] Significantly, Breandán Breathnach dedicated his seminal work, *Dancing in Ireland*, to the memory of Martin Talty.

Following Martin's death, Tom Munnelly, Dublin-born song collector and researcher, long-time supporter of the School and by then resident in the Miltown area, joined the committee, which was also strengthened by the return of Harry Hughes. For Hughes, it marked a welcome comeback following a period in which he had concentrated his efforts on the successful production of the School's 'sister' magazine, *Dal gCais*. The final addition to the committee came in the mid-eighties with the co-option of Eamon McGivney, a talented fiddle and accordion player from County Longford and long-time resident in the area.

The years from 1982 to 1988 can be seen as a transitional period for the School. Attendance figures continued to rise, reaching towards 700 by the end of the period. Junior Crehan and Paddy Joe McMahon were now the main links to the old musical culture of the area, and although the death of Breandán Breathnach in November 1985 was a considerable blow, NPU continued to support the School with undiminished enthusiasm.

Martin Talty introducing the whistle recital, 1978 (photo: Liam McNulty).

In 1982, the committee had decided to restructure the programme. Previously, lectures had been held at eight in the evening and the recitals at around half past three in the afternoon. However, this put terrible pressure on both the musicians – who, for the most part, were teaching until at least one o'clock – and the audience, many of who were class-attending students. Rearranging the recitals to a later time encouraged a greater number of musicians to attend.

Although CCÉ president de Brún had provided an official opening for the first school, this had been dropped in subsequent years. However, the official opening was reintroduced at the behest of Muiris Ó Rócháin:

> Apart from that first year, there were no openings for several years. The first man I asked to open it, I remember well, was Colm Ó Briain, director of the Arts Council in 1978. In selecting someone to open it, my guideline was this – someone who had given an artistic, creative or intellectual contribution to Irish life. We kept totally clear of politics. That would still be our guideline. Our first minister ever to open it this year for us, and the only reason is that she is from the county and, secondly,

Graveside tribute to Willie Clancy, late 1970s. Left to right: Seán Óg Potts, Seán Potts, Martin Talty (photo: WCSS Archive).

Eamon McGivney, WCSS director and co-director of the fiddle school, 1995.

she is the minister for culture, arts and the Gaeltacht [Síle de Valera].[19]

Traditional singing might have been expected to flourish at the School, particularly during the period when Tom Munnelly was a member of the committee.[20] However, in spite of Munnelly's great enthusiasm and penchant for introducing hitherto unknown local singers at the School, singing has never occupied a major place in the week's events.

Perhaps the achievements of the revised committee and the their supporters in NPU can be best summed up in this comment in *An Píobaire*:

> Willie Clancy Summer School 1987 was the most successful yet for the piping classes, of which there were 11. The number of pupils was 77, with a further 9 attending the workshop. The standard by which the classes are judged must be that of what the pupils feel about them. And the response was very positive. With classes, concerts, workshops and lunchtime recitals, this year's school was certainly the best yet.[21]

In 1987, it was decided to put the School and its committee on a more formal footing, with its transformation into a limited company. Up to that point, it might be said that the committee was a tight-knit group of people bound by a loose structure. Its members were close friends and, generally, enjoyed a shared philosophy on traditional culture, which meant that no formal constitution was needed.

In 1988, Tom Munnelly left the committee, leaving the remainder to carry on towards incorporation. From that point, the organisation assumed the structure that it enjoyed up to 1998: president, Junior Crehan; programme director and secretary, Muiris Ó Rócháin; administration director, Harry Hughes; music liaison, Eamon McGivney; and director, Seán Ó Duill. Dr Pádraig Ó hIrighle (Dr Patrick Hillery), former president of Ireland, is the patron. Since the death of Junior Crehan in 1998, the position of president has not been filled. Scoil Samhraidh Willie Clancy Teoranta (Willie Clancy Summer School Ltd) has the normal articles and schedules of association required by law.

Since 1988, few significant changes have been made, although in the late eighties accordion classes were added to the schedule. The programme now also includes two courses which are not dedicated to teaching practical skills. 'The Scope of Irish Music' was the brainchild of the late Breandán Breathnach, who thought it essential for young people coming to the music to have a rounded view of the tradition. However, for practical purposes, the class is scheduled to run parallel to the other classes, and although it attracts twenty or more students each year, most of those attending tend to be adult enthusiasts rather than youthful practitioners. The traditional singing workshop is conducted by Ian Lee and Brian Mullen and provides an overview of Ireland's singing traditions in both the English and Irish languages. Although both classes seem relatively small when compared with the instrumental and dancing classes, they are as large or larger than some of the instrumental classes of the early years.

While it might be claimed that the School's concentration on Ireland's traditional culture has helped in a general way, there had been no specific attempts to promote the Irish language at the School. However, starting in 2002, classes in basic Irish have been held daily and are open to all comers. This is part of an initiative by An Clár As Gaeilge, a community-based partnership that seeks to encourage the Irish language in County Clare.

* * *

The founders of the School envisaged that it would be structured around a core of three elements: practical classes, recitals and formal lectures. Although each element could operate independently of the others, in practice the three are generally tied fairly closely together, particularly the recitals and classes. In fact, the recitals generally consist of formalised musical demonstrations by members of the School's teaching staff. To some degree, the lectures enjoy an independent existence, as they are often delivered by specially invited visiting lecturers. The lecture topics, which are selected by the directors, cover a wide range of subjects and are intended to provide an overview of traditional culture in its widest sense. Hence, many topics are not directly connected with the School, west Clare or even Irish music. These have included topics such as 'The Reinterpretation of the Classical Pibroch'; 'The Music and Song Tradition of Brittany'; and 'From West Bengal to West Clare – In Pursuit of Traditional Song' (in spite of its title, not connected with west Clare).

Two lectures held in recent years – 'The Gaelic Song Tradition' and 'Gaelic Song and Music from the Isle of Skye' – demonstrate the close relationship that has developed with Scots Gaelic culture through connections with the Scottish festival *Ceolas*, which is supported by the Scottish National Gaelic Arts Project. In officially opening the School, Calum MacLean, founder of *Ceolas*, stated: 'The Willie Clancy Summer School is the model which we, in the Highlands and Islands of Scotland, view as the way forward for developing our traditional music and song.'[22]

A recent development has seen the introduction of seminars focusing on the hot topics of the day, and the large audiences for these events suggest that they could become a permanent fixture. Seminars have included: 'Change and Evolution in Irish Traditional Set and Step Dancing', with leading speakers Helen Brennan, Larry Lynch and Terence Moylan, chaired by Dr Catherine Foley; 'Trends in Traditional Music in the Late Twentieth Century', with leading speakers Professor Mícheál Ó Súilleabháin and Paddy Glackin, chaired by Fintan Vallely; and 'The Ó Riada Legacy – a Recollection', with Donal Ó Liatháin, Louis Marcus, Sean Potts and Peadar Ó Riada, chaired by Michael Tubridy.

The lectures and seminars are among the main justifications for the organiser's claim that, historically, the School has:

> . . . bridged the gap between the analytic and the instinctive: it revealed the possibility of combining an objective critique of the music in its historical and cultural contexts and the more immediate and primary functions of playing, dancing and singing. By linking formal scholarship with practical tuition and, at the same time, removing the element of competition as a reason for that tuition, the School has opened a wide spectrum of opportunities for traditional music followers and practitioners.[23]

Even though the practical classes, lectures and seminars enjoy relatively modest attendance, the School promotes many opportunities for interaction between the 'analytical' and the 'instinctive'. The majority of teachers see discussion of the wider aspects of traditional music as part of their teaching responsibilities, making strenuous efforts to imbue their students with the ethos of the tradition and to provide information on the transmission, function and development of traditional music, dance and song. The recitals, which are extremely well attended by students, also include a great deal of information about both the practice of the music and its practitioners. Even the apparently wall-to-wall music of the informal pub sessions is usually interspersed with anecdotes concerning the tradition and its practitioners.

As with so many other aspects of the School, it can be justifiably claimed that Ó Rócháin and Mac Mathúna had it just about right from the start. To quote Nicholas Carolan: 'I think the balance is about right in terms of different aspects, different experiences. I think that, if it's not proportionately more weighted towards participation and live experience, it could dry up. If it's only weighted towards the analytical, I don't think it would really work . . . I'd say they've got the balance about right, the elements of the mix and the balance of those elements.'[24]

Notes to Chapter 3

1 Recorded conversation between Muiris Ó Róchóin and Barry Taylor, Miltown Malbay, County Clare, 25 May 1998.

2 Séamus de Brún, 'Our Whole National Fibre Is Being Seriously Challenged', *Treoir*, series 5, no. 5 (1973), p. 20.

3 Anon., 'Activity Report', *Treoir*, series 5, no. 5 (1973), p. 3.

4 Muiris Ó Róchóin to Barry Taylor. (Fortunately, in this case, the strength of the principle was recognised and the Bank of Ireland made a contribution to organise set dancing classes as distinct from competitions.)

5 Editorial, *An Piobaire*, no. 14/15 (1974), p. 1. (I assume that this was an issue that overlapped 1973 and 1974 and that this piece was actually written in 1973. There is no doubt that the editor was referring to the forthcoming second School of 1974.)

6 As a general rule of thumb, the breakdown of registered participants is estimated as follows: set dancing 35 per cent; fiddle 25 per cent; whistle and flute 20 per cent; pipers 10 per cent; others 10 per cent.

7 Editorial, *An Piobaire*, no. 27 (1976), p. 1.

8 Recorded conversation between Harry Hughes and Barry Taylor, Mullagh, County Clare, 1 June 1998.

9 *Promoting the Music Market* (Miltown Malbay: 1995), section 3.1. This is a document formulated by the directors of the School to promote selective sponsorship; figures to 1998 updated during unrecorded conversation with Hughes, September 1998.

10 Recorded conversation between Brid O'Donohue (O'Brien) and Barry Taylor, Glandine, County Clare, 2 January 2001.

11 Muiris Ó Róchóin to Barry Taylor. In view of enormous growth in concertina playing in recent years and the association of the concertina with Clare musicians such as Elizabeth Crotty, Stack Ryan, John Kelly, Chris Droney, Packie Russell, etc., it may seem surprising that the instrument was not included in the original teaching programme. However, a concertina recital was featured from year 3 (1975), and featured most of the well-known players in County Clare. The year 1975 marked the start of an enormous revival of interest in the instrument prompted by the pioneering recording work of Englishman Neil Wayne of Free Reed. Wayne was responsible for the production of a number of LP releases on the joint Free Reed/Topic label, commencing in 1975. Although Hill was steadily building a reputation during the 1970s as Ireland's leading young player, his first commercial recording (with fiddle player Tony Linnane) was not released until 1979.

12 Muiris Ó Róchóin to Barry Taylor.

13 Confirmed during a recorded conversation between the writer and Michael Falsey, Quilty, County Clare, 23 October 2001.

14 See Helen Brennan, *The Story of Irish Dance* (Dingle: Brandon, 1999), pp. 159f, for a discussion of this issue.

15 E-mail from Terry Moylan to Barry Taylor, 22 November 2001.

16 Terry Moylan, ed., *Irish Dances* (Dublin: Na Píobairí Uilleann, 1984), p. viii; the name was borrowed from George Gavan's song 'Lanigan's Ball', written in 1860:
"For I spent three weeks at Brook's Academy
Learning new steps for Lanigan's Ball."

17 Harry Hughes to Barry Taylor.

18 *Ibid*.

19 Muiris Ó Róchóin to Barry Taylor. Others to have opened the School include: Tony McMahon (RTÉ); Joe O'Donovan; Adrian Munnelly (Arts Council); P. Joe Hayes (Tulla Céilí Band); Cathal Goan (Teilifís na Gaeilge); Paddy Glackin (RTÉ); and Irish Presidents Mary Robinson and Paddy Hillery.

20 Tom Munnelly has been collecting traditional songs since the mid-1960s and, since 1975, on behalf of the Department of Folklore, University College, Dublin. He has been a resident

of west Clare since the late 1970s and has an unrivalled knowledge of the singing traditions of the county.

21 Editorial, *An Piobaire*, no. 37 (1987).
22 Deirdre Hughes, *Small Town or World Capital?* (unpublished dissertation as part of BA (Hons.) Tourism Management, University of Wales Institute Cardiff. April 2001, p. 27.
23 Harry Hughes, ed., 'The Willie Clancy Summer School – Retrospectives'; *Dal gCais*, vol. 11 (1993), p. 7.
24 Recorded conversation between Nicholas Carolan and Barry Taylor, Dublin, 24 April 1998.

Thursday

SEÁN MCKEON IS the son of the celebrated piper Gay McKeon. Perhaps the youngest teacher at the School, Seán is putting four equally youthful students through their paces on a difficult reel, 'The Scholar'. 'This is one of those tunes that allows you to put a lot of yourself in. It's tricky enough, and you have to get it right before you can start to add individual touches.'

Seán McKeon, 2001.

Seán plays the first phrase of the tune and asks one of the students to play it after him. The youngster is struggling with his bellows, and Seán takes a look. The bellows is leaking air from a joint, and Seán is unable to effect an immediate repair but advises the student to give it attention at the first opportunity. The tune goes around the class, with each student demonstrating a high degree of proficiency. A lady with a small child enters and asks whether they can listen to the music. Seán smiles and nods. Eventually, Seán is satisfied that his charges have mastered the basics. As lunchtime approaches, he gives one final and masterful demonstration of 'The Scholar' before asking, 'What now? I suppose you all want "Colonel Fraser's"?' The classmates grin in unison, and Seán sighs before launching into the tune.

Sorcha Ní Mhuire (right) and student, piping class, 2001.

The accordion was a fairly late addition to the School's instrumental reper-toire. However, it is well served, with tuition provided by players such as Joe Burke, Ann Conroy and Conor Keane. Conor's class is an outpost of the School's empire and is situated in the Salesian Youth Centre out past Span-ish Point. The class covers a wide age range, with several of the older mem-bers coming from the UK. Conor faces a particular challenge as accordions can be tuned in a variety of different configurations. 'Generally, I play an accordion on which one row is tuned in D and the other in D#. However, most members of my class use the more common B/C tuning. Each tuning has its own advantages, and fortunately I can play in both.'

Conor starts the morning by playing through a jig and asking the class to play with him. 'OK, let's see if we can add some ornamentation to this tune – we can try a triplet.' Conor demonstrates a triplet and suggests that class members should mark their musical notation to show where this might be used. 'Don't forget that this type of ornamentation can become very boring if it's used all the time, so it's best used sparingly.'

Conor Keane (centre left) and his accordion class, 2001.

Chapter 4

The Teaching of Traditional Music and Dance

I T IS, PERHAPS, not surprising that traditional music and dance should have found no place in formal education in Ireland in colonial times. From the earliest days, the colonists considered that any aspect of Irish traditional culture could pose a threat to their rule, and as early as the fourteenth century, cultural manifestations such as the Irish language were banned. In the event, it is hardly surprising that the promotion of Irish culture – in its many and varied forms – fell to the nationalist movement. However, it is surprising that following the establishment of the Irish Free State in 1922 no serious attempt should have been made to include traditional music, song or dance in the curricula of schools until comparatively recently.[1]

The older generations of musicians managed quite well without the competitions, cups and certificates thought necessary by many 'revivalists' to stimulate interest. As Jimmy Ward, a long-time resident in Miltown and a member of both the Kilfenora and the Laichtin Naofa Céilí Bands, commented: 'In my youth, you were strictly judged by the way in which you played for the set. Nothing else mattered. . .'[2] In the Kilfenora of the early decades of the twentieth century, there were two possible verdicts on a musician's playing. If a musician was good, the saying was, 'They'd put you out through the rafters.' But if the performance was not up to scratch, they were damned with the statement, 'They'd stick you to the ground!'

However, there is no doubt that, historically, instrumental skills were not always acquired in a totally haphazard fashion. Although the evidence for musical training being systematically organised on a craft basis is a little thin, there are suggestions of a system in which youngsters were apprenticed to master musicians. Writing in the 1820s, William Carleton, the novelist and folklorist, suggests that some kind of training was available for budding musicians at least into the early part of nineteenth century:

> A fiddle is procured for him by his parents, if they are able, and, if not, a subscription is made up among their friends and neighbours to buy him one. All the family, with tears in their eyes, then kiss and take leave of him; and his mother, taking him by the hand, leads him, as had been previously arranged, to the best fiddler in the neighbourhood, with whom he is left as an apprentice. There is generally no fee required, but he is engaged to hand his master all the money he can make at dances, from the time he is proficient enough to play at them.[3]

The pastimes of the rural populace were to be rudely disrupted by the massive social changes resulting from the onset of famine in the 1840s. In the midst of such upheaval, it seems improbable that the rural population could have supported professional musicians and dancers when they themselves were clothed in rags, struggling to keep a roof over their heads and starving to death. However, the accounts of Garret Barry's piping apprenticeship, probably as late as the 1860s, suggests that the practice may have lingered on in parts of the country, such as County Clare.

The last decades of the nineteenth century were a time of great change in rural Ireland. Although the mid-century years of famine had resulted in untold hardship and misery, conditions of life began to slowly improve. Although extremely limited in their scope, the Land Acts of 1870 and 1881 resulted in improvements in living conditions for many. The meagre one-room dwellings of previous generations gradually gave way to houses with separate kitchens, which meant that dancing – formerly a mainly outdoor pursuit – could be practised in the family home.

It is probable that the same social and economic forces promoted a shift away from the paid (albeit extremely poorly) musicians and dance teachers of the eighteenth and early nineteenth century. This is likely to have had an effect on the way the music was played. Firstly, the provision of music by local musicians is the likely source of the profusion of highly localised styles that are characteristic of Irish music. Secondly, it might be argued that, as the musicians were not reliant on the dancers for their daily bread, they would be less bound than the professional to serve up the strict brand of music demanded by the dancers.

From this period, tales of itinerant musicians and dance teachers of the eighteenth and nineteenth century begin to be replaced by accounts of teachers plying their trade from fixed locations. Although at a slightly later date, perhaps the two periods spent in west Clare by teacher Pat Barron, a native of west Limerick, serve to demonstrate the changing times. When Barron first came to Clare around the time of the 1914–1918 war, he plied his trade around the parishes of the western seaboard in the fashion of the itinerant master. However, around 1933, he reappeared and, after marrying a woman from Mullagh, settled in the area. As Junior Crehan recalls, his activities during the latter period seemed to be very well organised: 'When he came back in 1933, he held three schools in the area: one was in a disused house in Mullagh, another in an unoccupied house belonging to Peter Daffy in Doonogan, and the third in Michael Looney's house in Mount Scott. To the disused house people brought turf for the fire and oil for the lamps.'[4]

* * *

The early years of the twentieth century saw the introduction of formal education for musicians and dancers. Not surprisingly, in the final decades of British rule, such programmes were not provided by the state education system but by nationalist organisations. The driving force behind the majority of these initiatives was the Gaelic League (*Conradh na Gaeilge*). The League was founded in 1893 with the objective of constructing a 'new' Ireland based on its Gaelic past – or perhaps we should say more accurately, a Gaelic past as reconstructed and interpreted by its followers.

In May 1897, the League launched the *feis cheoil* in Dublin. This was a competitive event modelled on the Welsh *eisteddfod*.[5] Participants were expected to choose their pieces for performance from a set repertoire and were assessed according to standards set by the organisers.

Similar events could be found throughout the country, particularly in areas with a strong League base, such as Miltown Malbay. But, despite early enthusiasm, the *feis cheoil* gradually ran out of steam in the 1920s. Although the movement enjoyed only a relatively short-lived popularity among traditional musicians, it did inspire the notion that some might become concert performers. However, Padraig Pearse argued that peasant musicians 'are of the countrysides and for the countrysides', while musicologist Carl Hardebeck declared in 1911 that '. . . the traditional singer in the habit of singing in the kitchen . . . has no business to be dragged on to the concert platform'.[6]

The perceived failure of most of the participants to meet the mark set by the *feis* organisers (few of whom had any real knowledge of traditional music) led to demands for formal musical education in schools. This was a belief fundamental to the thinking behind the *feis cheoil* movement and, to a great extent, provided the rationale for its objectives.

In 1929, through the founding of *An Coimisiún le Rincí Gaelacha* (Irish Dance Commission), the League began to force dancing into a strait jacket of rules and procedures from which it is yet to escape. It also invented a number of dances that had no foundation in the Irish tradition. Joe O'Donovan commented:

> . . . when they came to dance, they found they were dancing sets and quadrilles which carried names like Lancers, Caledonians, Alberts, Victorias and so on, ergo, these were English dances, . . . and they had to invent new dances which they called céilí dances. People such as Bean Uí Curráin, who was secretary of the Gaelic League in Limerick, invented the Walls of Limerick and the Siege of Ennis. An t-Athair Ó Glannagáin invented the Fairy Reel and so on. Later, Finnán Mac Colum and Tomás Ó Feanalaigh collected some of the older dances, which were introduced into the new repertory of dances.[7]

The late nineteenth century interest in traditional music prompted a number of activities, such as the founding of the Dublin Pipers' Club around 1900. Although the Civil War put an end to its gatherings, it was revived by Leo Rowsome in 1936, and his presiding genius enabled the art and craft of pipe playing and making to be passed on to future generations.

In January and February 1951, representatives of the Pipers' Club met the organisers of *Feis Lár na hÉireann* (a Gaelic League *feis* that had been held in Mullingar for many years). It was decided to organise jointly a musical event in Mullingar in May over the Whit weekend (later to be named the *fleadh cheoil*). In turn, this led to the election of the first standing committee of *Cumann Ceoltóirí na hÉireann* on 14 October 1951, which assumed the now familiar title *Comhaltas Ceoltóirí Éireann* on 6 January 1952. Its aim was to promote traditional music and to arrest the decline in its popularity. Unlike in the later years of the nineteenth century, there is no doubt that the middle years of the twentieth century had seen traditional music descend to a parlous state, and this contributed a sense of urgency to the actions of CCÉ, promoting an air of revivalist zeal in many members. Some in the fledgling organisation saw its activities simply as a way of bringing musicians together. Others, however, perceived indifference and even antagonism in both the 'establishment' and the population at large to the culture and tradition of Ireland. This helped promote a philosophy that was highly reminiscent of that of the Gaelic League and which, to this day, underpins the aims of CCÉ: '. . . although the ordinary people of Ireland loved traditional music, the thousands of traditional musicians in the country were largely unappreciated in *popular social and intellectual circles*.' [My italics][8]

In its early days, CCÉ was welcomed by traditional musicians, and when a branch was formed in the early fifties in Miltown, the local musicians did not hesitate to join in its ranks. But as time passed, musicians such as Willie Clancy began to note its decline into mediocrity:

> In my opinion, CCÉ has done considerable work for the music. Certainly, at the beginning, it could be regarded as having given a much-needed injection to the revival of interest in music. But, in those years, *fleadh cheoil* were all that they were intended to be: gatherings of dedicated Irish musicians playing to true followers of the music. Afterwards, unfortunately, the undesirable element crept in and we were subject to an abuse of tambourines and guitars and a display of showmanship with little or no sincerity. This type of attitude is not good enough if we are to preserve what's valuable.[9]

As in the *feis cheoil* movement, CCÉ has seen competition as the principle stimulus for reviving interest in the music, and, in an uncanny echo of the early objectives of the Gaelic League, its teaching programme has become increasingly integrated into the state system. It is now validated by a Traditional Irish Music examination, promoted jointly by the Royal Irish Academy of Music and CCÉ. This was launched by Irish President Mary McAleese at Dublin Castle on 14 December 1998 and extended to cover the United Kingdom in 2000. The examination enables traditional musicians to progress through the elementary, junior and senior cycles, and have their proficiency tested and certified at each stage. Performance is assessed by an official body of experts at a distance from the context of transmission, all of which leaves little scope for individual creativity, judgement or innovation.

Launching the new examination structure, CCÉ announced:

> For the last fifty years or so, practitioners of traditional music have been able to achieve recognition for their achievements through the extensive CCÉ Fleadhanna Cheoil competitions at County, Provincial and All-Ireland levels. The Irish Traditional Music examination includes both performance and theoretical aspects (for example, sources of tunes, regional styles, profiles of musicians, and musical events). Therefore, this new examination will enable a greater number of musicians to obtain formal recognition for their efforts, while also broadening their knowledge and understanding of the tradition.[10]

Thus, as Breandán Breathnach and his colleagues shrewdly observed as early as the 1960s, practices arising from performance in competition, with its inevitable emphasis on a common repertoire, precise standards, agreed evaluative criteria and uniformity are enshrined in the philosophy of CCÉ and have become critical to its teaching of traditional music, song and dance.

* * *

When Muiris Ó Rócháin and Séamus Mac Mathúna were planning the first Willie Clancy Summer School, the majority of their potential students were young people, of whom a significant percentage were non-Irish. Irrespective of origin or nationality, many were coming to Irish music for the first time. Significantly, in the period before the rise of interest in set dancing, traditional dance music had increasingly become an entertainment for a listening audience.

Teaching outside the ranks of CCÉ was largely informal and generally followed traditional patterns and practices. As a practising teacher, Ó Rócháin knew that the most common and often most effective form of teaching involves simple demonstration and, reinforced by Mac Mathúna's practical experience, resolved that this should be the general method employed by the School. As they journeyed into the unknown, they were sure of two things: that there was a significant demand for tuition in the playing of music and that, with the passing of time, the pool of musicians from the older generation would dwindle.

In an interview with Willie Clancy conducted by Muiris Ó Rócháin and Harry Hughes in 1972 – almost certainly, the last interview given before his death – Willie outlined the advice he would give to young musicians:

> Get a grasp of the Gaelic tongue and develop a love for it. Go to the Gaeltacht and the old people who have [it] and learn it. I feel that a knowledge of our language is essential if you are to express the true spirit of our music. And, as the saying goes, 'Don't settle for the skim milk when the cream is at hand.' Apart from that, have patience; learn to walk before you run. You might have a flair for the music, you might think you're good at it and you might be tempted to plunge ahead without perfecting your technique. Well, it might be in your head but your fingers will let you down. So, start playing early and develop your technique with patience, practice and perseverance.[11]

In *Folk Music and Dances of Ireland*, published in 1971 and still the most authoritative work on the subject, Breandán Breathnach, a close friend of Willie's, states that '. . . there is only one way of becoming a traditional player or singer, and that is by listening to genuine material played in a traditional manner.'.

John Kelly (senior) used to tell his fiddle students that once you have the tune in your head, bringing it out on the fiddle would follow.[12] Perhaps fortunately for his young and usually impatient students, John didn't say how long either process might take, but, of course, in the rural Ireland of John's youth, time was not so important. In addition, in the age of the electronic media, it is difficult to appreciate that, in John's youth, virtually the only music to be heard in rural Ireland was that which is now referred to reverentially as 'traditional music'. Thus, the experience of John Kelly and his contemporaries was very different from that of the young people of twenty-first century Ireland, whose daily musical experience is more likely to come from the transmitters of a commercial radio station than from the singing of a neighbour.

Ó Rócháin and Mac Mathúna wanted to emulate the practices of the communities for whom passing on their traditions of music and dance had been an ongoing process. Although the pool of local musicians from the older generation had declined significantly, they believed that there were certain core values and practices that had underpinned the culture of *clachan* society throughout the country. Thus, they felt that they were free to recruit

John Kelly, Sr, and student, early 1980s (photo: Liam McNulty).

from the traditional music community at large. This was to prove vital to the survival of the School as the ranks of the bearers of the local tradition continued to decline.

In the communities surrounding Miltown, Martin Talty was typical of the relatively small number of musicians who had struggled tenuously to hold on to their heritage through the lean years of the forties and who had been eager to pass it on to future generations. Martin's priority was:

> . . . to continue the work which was Willie Clancy's lifelong passion, the construction and maintenance of the *uilleann* pipes and pipe reeds . . . [T]he committee behind the *Scoil Éigse* were determined that a workshop where young pipers could study and try the arts and skills of pipe and reed making should be the focal point . . . with [other] activities including instruction in whistle and fiddle playing and *sean-nós* singing. . .[13]

Ironically, the main motivation for the launch of the School – the passing of one of the most significant of local tradition bearers – was an event that significantly reduced the capacity to pass on the local culture to future generations. Although traditional music and dance had survived longer in west Clare than in many other parts of Ireland and was perceived as healthy from outside the locality, its future was uncertain. Many of its most competent practitioners, such as Bobby Casey of Annagh, Tommy McCarthy of Kilmihil, Joe Ryan of Inagh and John Joe Healy of Quilty, had emigrated in the early 1950s, and younger recruits such as Brid O'Donohue were thin on the ground. Much of the enthusiasm engendered in the fifties was ebbing, and with the notable exception of Marty Malley's occasional ventures, the country house dance had passed into near oblivion.

By the seventies, the *céilí* band boom was well past its peak. Many of its most notable practitioners had transferred to smaller groups in order to cater for the growing pub lounge trade. In west Clare, such groups included the Bannermen (with Michael Sexton, Jimmy Ward and singer P.J. Murrihy) and the Leon Group from Quilty, which included the fine piper and flute player Michael Falsey. Although these groups often contained a strong core of traditional musicians, the demand was for variety, and jigs, reels and hornpipes alternated with modern popular music. In addition, the late fifties and sixties witnessed the inexorable rise of an Irish popular music phenomenon, the showband – a trend that was to last until the traditional music revival of the late sixties and early seventies.

As time passed, the number of musicians who could be truly described as representatives of the musical cultures of specific communities was to decline alarmingly. By the year 2001, from Muiris Ó Róchán's list of 'exemplary' musicians, all but Peadar O'Loughlin and Joe Ryan had passed on, and only Peadar had remained in the locality.

The relationship that developed between local musicians such as Willie Clancy, Martin Talty, Paddy Joe McMahon and Junior Crehan and the outsiders (including some with a distinctly non-Irish pedigree) in the 1960s and 1970s appears to have been symbiotic, with each group clearly deriving benefit from the encounter. As a public rather than private forum, the public house facilitated a level of communication between them that would not have been possible if the music had remained within the home.

Music making helps to create and define identity, so, for the indigenous west Clare musicians, the fact that someone was a musician was much more important than the fact that he or she was Dutch, British or American. This goes a long way to explaining why, generally and often to their surprise, struggling fiddle, flute and pipe playing foreigners have found a ready welcome both in County Clare and in the other parts of Ireland where the tradition has survived.

As the following comment indicates, the School appears to have managed to imbue its latter-day recruits with much of the same attitude: 'My favourite thing about the Willie Week is the multicultural attitude. I went last year and played sessions with Germans, Swiss, Czechs, Swedes, Americans, Irish, Scottish, South Africans, and people from just about any other country under the sun. I was amazed at the camaraderie and the great friends I found.'[14]

* * *

It has always been the intention of the School's organisers to recruit teachers of the highest quality: 'All we can do with the School is provide the best available and have the type of people available, like P.J. Hayes, Junior Crehan, Peter O'Loughlin, Martin Talty, Bobby Casey, Joe Ryan . . . You have them there as sort of the linchpin. All you can do, I suppose to a certain extent, is set up an example.'[15]

But finding suitable replacements for the older generation has not always proved easy. Although many of the younger generation are fine musicians and sometimes perhaps better prepared for a teaching role than their predecessors, inevitably, with the passage of time, they are moving further away from the roots of the tradition.

However, it is important to realise that the formal classes are only one aspect of the learning process. As in all educational processes, interaction

Paddy Canny and Peadar O'Loughlin, 1995.

with fellow students is extremely important in the development of skills and knowledge, and many students develop lasting relationships. In addition, students are encouraged to attend the many recitals and lectures, all of which contribute to a greater understanding of the culture. In fact, the School provides the opportunity for participants to immerse themselves completely in traditional music for a week. However, it does require a fairly high degree of self-motivation for the student to avail of all the opportunities on offer – a personal skill not always so highly developed in the younger students. In passing, it must be remarked that full participation also requires a great deal of stamina!

Even though the programme states that 'there are no classes for beginners in instruments other than pipes', beginners are also accepted in three other categories: set dancing, the traditional singing workshop and 'The Scope of Irish Music'. Although the latter two classes have relatively low enrolments (usually, two to three dozen per class), dancing classes are very heavily subscribed and often contain a hefty percentage of beginners.

Two whistle students practise during the mid-morning break, 2002.

Although the School's organisers had set their sights on a format that promoted all aspects of traditional music, piping has always occupied a unique place in its activities. However, the fiddle classes represent the largest individual instrumental group, while dancers – both set and individual – now comprise up to 50 per cent of all students.

* * *

From its relatively humble beginnings, NPU has grown into a sizeable and influential organisation and can be said to a truly representative association for all *uilleann* pipers. It has impressive permanent headquarters[16] and publishes an informative journal, An *Píobaire*, five times annually.

NPU eschews involvement with competition, choosing to concentrate on education, training and research. Since the second year of the School (1974), NPU has been responsible for piping activities. There is an impressive menu awaiting the piping student, including piping classes (around fifteen in 2002), daily workshops for reed making and general pipe maintenance, specialised recitals and workshops for players, and a daily concert of piping, with performers selected by NPU. NPU also maintains the School's 'official' shop in the Community Hall, which sells piping accoutrements as well as a wide range of books, records, CDs and videos – plus the widely popular Willie Clancy Summer School T-shirt. Full details of all official piping activities taking place at the School are contained in a separate leaflet published by NPU.

In addition to lessening the burden for the often hard-pressed officials of the School, this has led to its development as the leading forum of *uilleann* piping. The importance of the School to NPU is emphasised by the holding of the annual general meeting of Na *Píobairí Uilleann Teoranta* (Limited) during the week of school. In fact, the NPU relocates to Miltown for the week, and unlike all other instrumentalists, *uilleann* pipers rest safely in the fold of an organisation dedicated specifically to their needs.

Due to the intricacies of the pipes and the involvement of NPU, piping classes are organised rather differently from those of all the other instruments. Students are encouraged to enrol with NPU prior to the commencement of the School in order to facilitate student grading and the allocation of teaching staff. While all students of other instruments are graded on the first Monday morning of the School week, pipers can be graded by NPU in Dublin prior to the week. Of course, it is not feasible to grade all pipers prior to the School, and facilities are also open for grading on the first Monday. In addition, the pipes are the only instrument for which beginners' classes are provided. The provision of this facility emphasises the historical role played by the School in the revival of piping, as in the early years, many (if not most) piping students had little or no prior experience. Finally, the reed making and maintenance workshop are unique to the pipes.

Of course, teaching is at the heart of all activities and, excepting the special facilities noted above, follows much the same general pattern practised for the other instruments taught at the School. The following account from Thomas Johnson of Sweden provides a flavour of the classes:

> I've been going to the summer school since 1996, taking piping classes. The piping classes are not overcrowded, usually between five and seven pupils. I've attended classes taught by Al Purcell (R.I.P.), Pat Mitchell and Tom Clarke, and we all received a very large amount of individual attention.

A young student in Sorcha Ní Mhuire's piping class, 2001.

Pat Mitchell told us that he wasn't going to teach tunes, as we could get these just as well back home. He wanted to teach us piping techniques, so, Pat being a great man for the tight triplets, we proceeded to tie our fingers in knots that week. It was a great week: Pat is quite blunt and doesn't mince words, but is also very entertaining and fun.

Tom Clarke's class was also technique based. Tom would pick a simple tune ('The Heather Breeze', 'Dusty Miller' etc.) that most of us already knew or that was easy to pick up, and then teach us techniques to use within the tune. As there are only five or so of us, there is no chance of slacking off, and one has to pay attention. Like Al Purcell and Pat, Tom seems to possess an enormous patience. Frankly, I don't know how the piping teachers manage six days of piping pupils, squeaking and squawking, often on loud, out of tune chanters, and yet still keep their composure, at least for the most part. I always wonder what do they do the week after. Perhaps they all go off to a retreat somewhere and sit in silence for a week.

As far as piping classes go, I think the quality is still there. I did hear some grumblings about the pedagogical status of one of the younger alumni. But I'm convinced that the piping classes, master classes, the piping workshop and afternoon recitals and, last but not least, the tea breaks, where one gets to talk and discuss pipes and piping, are quite simply amazing, both in value for money and in the knowledge that's imparted.[17]

* * *

Pipers are exceedingly fortunate – or extremely farsighted – in having an organisation to serve their individual needs and sadly, for the School at least, there are no national equivalents to NPU for other instruments. Individual teachers organise and conduct their activities under the general authority of the School's directors.

Since far and away the largest group of students are those playing fiddles, we can take this group as being generally representative of the other instruments. The 'fiddle school' is headed by John Kelly, ever present at the School and son of one of the original teachers, and Eamon McGivney. To John and Eamon falls the unenviable task of ensuring that upwards of 400 fiddle players of widely varying levels of ability are placed in classes appropriate to their needs.

Tom Clarke, 1995.

There is no doubt that the relatively unstructured format of the School can pose problems for students accustomed to the rigours of orthodox education. This is particularly the case with younger students, who, not surprisingly, sometimes lack the self-discipline and motivation required to achieve their best from this fairly loosely structured system.

The first Monday morning of the School might, to a stranger, resemble a badly organised horse fair, as the organisers attempt to match the mass of students of varying levels of ability with appropriate teachers. However, contrary to immediate appearances, the task is carried out with remarkable efficiency and good humour, and completed by lunchtime, although some students will transfer later in the week.

The organisers are not helped by some students wanting to be placed in the class of a particularly well-known musician. As someone commented, 'You try telling someone who has come to attend the Martin Hayes or Brendan McGlinchey class that they can't come in!' This situation is exacerbated when the student in question has travelled from Sweden, or even Australia or Japan.

John Kelly, co-director of the fiddle school and son of John Kelly, Sr, 1997.

Unfortunately, not everyone can get the teacher he or she wants, and some students are naturally going to feel let down, but it says much for the tact and understanding of the organisers that such disappointments are relatively few in number. The satisfaction of the overwhelming majority of students is confirmed by around 70 per cent of students returning for a second time. However, the fact that even a relatively small number of students leave the School dissatisfied with their week's work should not be dismissed lightly. In most cases, this is due to being placed in an inappropriate class:

> [One student] was extremely disappointed when he was placed in an 'advanced' whistle class mostly consisting of young kids who couldn't play a D scale. . . . the class could spend a day on learning the notes of a polka (which I think any average musician would get after listening to it only a couple of times). I think that the focus shouldn't be on tunes, but what can 'be done' with them. The time spent on 'learning' the tune takes too much time.[18]

Problems relating to individual class allocation largely arise from trying to squeeze as much as possible into the week. But, given the nature of the School and the voluntary teaching staff, its is hard to see a practical alternative to the present system. Even in the case of NPU's highly structured piping activities, although prior enrolment and grading are encouraged, the majority of students enrol and are graded during the first morning of the School. The alternative of a more thorough grading process would eat further into tuition time and would be unlikely to prove popular with the majority of students. In addition, the composition of the classes is fairly fluid. Whether prompted by the teacher or their own judgement, students can, and often do, move to classes other than those to which they were initially allocated.

However, problems can still occur and can lead to near heartbreak for the student who is placed in a class either above or below his/her ability. In his first year as a fiddle teacher at the School, Brendan McGlinchey encountered a difficult, but perhaps not untypical, problem:

> This particular student came in late on Monday or Tuesday morning, because he'd been to a couple of other classes and it wasn't working out. He couldn't speak English very well, and he was a very poor fiddle player: when I asked him to play a tune for me, he just barely played the 'Irish Washerwoman' . . . I thought from that moment when I heard him, [that] this is problematical, . . . I didn't want to push him out of

the door because he'd fall from the landing. Where would he go? He'd been to two or three classes before that.

So, he was coming in to me, he was almost looking at me and saying, 'Sanctuary!' . . . I was looking at him from the point of view of being a foreign visitor to these shores and coming with a fiddle to learn music, and I thought, if I had anything to teach him at all, I'd willingly give it to him. . . . I said to him, 'You can't be a problem in the class because I must go ahead. You can't be a hindrance to the rest.'

And he said, 'Let me stay one day.' I said, 'Certainly, but don't struggle. Just listen and see what you can pick up.' And, of course, I was talking to him like this in an open classroom, and the rest were listening. He stayed, and at the end of the day, you could see the brow furrowing, deeper and deeper and the eyes standing out in his head. On Wednesday morning, he came in and, even the way he was holding the fiddle, it was uptight, all tight and the muscles in his whole body were taut. I'd go to him and I'd say, 'Are you all right?' 'Yes, yes.' And you could see that when we were playing one tune, he would play possibly three notes

Brendan McGlinchey and students, 1994.

in eight bars and that's all. I said to him, 'If you're not getting it, don't bother with rushing to get it. Just listen to it, absorb the melody, and after a while the melody will be transmitted, will be implanted, it will be in your mind, and it will gradually come down to your fingers. Give yourself time. If you rush it, you will only make mistakes.'

And he listened and he went away. He told me on Thursday morning that, on Wednesday afternoon, he'd gone on to the rocks and he nearly threw the fiddle into the sea, but he had a little tape recorder with him, and he listened and he practised and he listened and he practised. And, on Thursday morning, he came in and, on Wednesday, he had said, 'I don't know if I should be here or not. I don't know if I should be in another classroom, or if I should just go into Miltown and just sit in the middle of the town. . . . but I listened and I played and I think I am progressing!' So, he played a little bit for me, very scratchily, but great progress.

And we were going out in the evening . . . and didn't I spot him in the middle of the street in Miltown with the fiddle under his chin, playing away with a group of other people! Obviously delighted with what he was doing and had the confidence and the courage to go into a group of people, playing away, and, on Friday, by God, was he happy![19]

The teachers in the fiddle classes and for most of the other instruments generally rely on teaching by example. The system can be characterised as being empirical, that is, based on observation and practice rather than academic and based on theory. Most of the teachers try to provide instruction in traditional technique through the teaching of specific tunes, rather than exercises – a method demonstrably rooted in local tradition.

We can find a good example of this half a dozen miles or so from Miltown itself. Fiddle player Michael Downes of Doonogan, who was a pupil of the late Junior Crehan of Bonavella in the 1930s, described the method employed: 'At first, Junior would finger them [tunes] out to you – by time, he'd just play them . . . and you might play them away with him, you know, all be depending how quick you were to pick up.'[20]

Another example of the traditional method of teaching is provided by J.P. Shannon from Kilfarboy. His teacher was Pat Barron, and although Barron was primarily a dance teacher, he was willing to turn his hand to music teaching. J.P. acquired some thirty tunes from him, at the price of one shilling per tune! As J.P. recalls:

He'd call out the notes one by one out of the tune... and he had no fiddle or anything . . . he'd have them all in his head. He'd know where the third finger [should be on] the third string, and the second finger on the second string. . . . He'd call the tune. He'd [also] show you and play three or four notes and he'd make you play 'em after, same as ABC. He'd make you start with a down bow stroke and finish with an up bow stroke and he'd tell you where there was a slur.[21]

Although the method described by Michael Downes and J.P. Shannon was effective, it was fairly lengthy and placed considerable emphasis on the ability of the pupil to memorise both technique and repertoire. It is, perhaps, most effective when the pupil has regular access to the teacher and when the teacher/pupil relationship extends over a good period of time, a luxury not enjoyed by students at the School. In order to overcome this problem, students are encouraged to bring tape recorders. In general, like the musicians of old, the teachers at the School tend to 'finger out' tunes to students. Depending on the preference of the individual teacher, tunes might also be written either on a black/whiteboard for students to copy or distributed in sheet form.

Fiddle player Michael Ardern, originally from England but for some time resident in County Sligo, gives us a flavour of life in a class with Martin Hayes:

Martin was always averse to any vetting, *Comhaltas* style, as to who attended his class, and so there would always be a complete cross-section, from eight and nine year olds through students in their middle years, many from the States or the UK, and a few geriatrics like myself. What was on offer was six mornings of three-hour classes. Martin would usually start off by just sitting and playing maybe for twenty minutes, doodling so to speak, and getting warmed up. This would often be the most inspiring part, as you would be sitting right next to him, appreciating all the nuances of tone and dynamics and rhythm, and absorbing subliminally the bowing patterns and much else that you couldn't consciously analyse. You realised how inadequately one-dimensional is even the best quality recording. Out of all this he would pick on a tune and go through it slowly, exploring all its intricacies and meanderings until we had it in our heads, at which point we would hands on and play it ourselves. Mostly everybody would be at a level where this presented no problem, and very few wouldn't be able to play it through competently after a few minutes.

I suppose that Martin has identified certain areas on which he concentrates. Prominent would be the need to free oneself from habitual bowing patterns in order to gain a greater freedom with interpretation.

This he advised to do by taking a tune and bowing it from one end of the bow to the other, not changing direction until you run out of bow. This is actually quite difficult to do, as it goes completely against the grain. Another area would be concentrating on the finest nuance of each individual note. It came as a revelation to me at that first class that volume is not related to pressure but to bow speed, and that the dynamics of the music are produced by varying the speed of the bow, even during the course of one note.

Another area would be rhythm and 'lift'. Perhaps this is the most difficult of all areas to teach, as it is purely instinctive. Examples would be given of playing on the beat, before the beat and after the beat, and the different feel this gives the music. Martin always emphasised the importance of being physically comfortable and relaxed while playing and allowing the music to be felt in the feet and indeed through the whole body.

A third area, perhaps the one that interested me the least, would be improvisation and development of a tune. This is not to find fault with Martin, but is simply a reflection of my innate conservatism. Martin sometimes goes to places that are fine for him but wouldn't fit me!

One of the joys of being with Martin is that there is no sense that he is sticking to any previously worked out structure, other than to get across a few basic and major points such as those described. But there is a refreshing spontaneity and openness to whatever is the inspiration of the moment.

The second part of the class after the break would usually be devoted to chat about the music and general philosophy. Sometimes this could be completely inspiring, and other times you might actually find yourself beginning to nod off, wishing he'd just play. [But] it is a joy to hear Martin reminisce about the older generation of east Clare players and their approach to the music. Another favourite topic is the state of the music and where it's heading – guaranteed to be both stimulating and entertaining.

At the first workshop I attended with Martin, he brought in *sean-nós* singer Áine Ní Dhonnacha and a dancer, Mick Mulkerrins, to demonstrate a couple of things. Firstly, interpreting the music on an instrument as if it were sung, with all the nuances implied; and, secondly, the way that the rhythm is rooted in the dance – and the interconnection of music and dance. There was also a visit from Junior [Crehan] and Bobby [Casey], which was very memorable, particularly as Junior told a few of his stories.

Martin teaches somehow from the top, but, just occasionally, I find myself wishing he would be more pupil-centred. For example, to work with a student as in a master-class, where the student would have a crack at a tune, and Martin might just occasionally, on a one to one basis, pinpoint how that individual player might perhaps do things differently. But I suppose that's a difficult area, and in any case, Martin is always urging people to 'find their own voice' rather than be a carbon copy of somebody else. Then I guess that quite a few students, particularly the younger ones, would be wishing that they could spend more time playing instead of sitting listening to Martin talking, with their fiddles immobile in their hands. But I suppose that there is the rest of the year for playing, and you don't easily avail yourself of this quality of input. I do think that some of the younger ones might have been happier in a class where they spent more time simply learning tunes and getting hands-on experience.

Bobby Casey (foreground) and Junior Crehan play for Máire O'Keefe's class, 1992.

One last point: the inspiration of the class doesn't stop when you leave Miltown but continues right through the year. Thanks to recording technology, it is almost as good as having Martin's presence in your living room.[22]

The following account from Philippe Varlet (born in France but now living in the USA) provides an excellent synopsis of the experience of so many:

There were only two [fiddle classes] then; beginners, taught by John Kelly Jr., and advanced, taught by John Kelly Sr. and Bobby Casey. I decided to take the advanced class since I had been playing for a couple of years. Right there in the hall where we were signing up was a piper who had just gotten delivery of his full set from Brian Howard. As I learned from talking to him a bit, he was a Danish schoolteacher, and he came to Ireland every summer to learn to play, as he had no one to play with at home and only practised with records there.

My fiddle class had perhaps a dozen students. Myself and an Australian man were the only non-Irish there, as well as the oldest (I was 23), the Irish being all kids or teenagers. We were asked to introduce ourselves and play something. I don't remember what I played, but it must have been good enough because they didn't throw me out . . . I was very impressed by the playing of the Irish teenager sitting next to me. His name was Dermot McLaughlin! I even thought: why isn't he teaching? He sounds much better than the old scratchy guys with fingers like tree stumps. Of course, my perspective on this has changed a bit since. Later that week, Dermot would record a great tape full of tunes for me. Manus Lunny, whom I had met at a session, came with us to a prefab school building. Right after we started recording, someone outside began to mow the grass. I still have the tape, and you can hear the lawnmower's engine getting closer and then moving away during certain tunes.

I remember two tunes we were taught in fiddle class. The first was a jig called 'Bobby Casey's'. John Kelly Sr. did all of the talking and demonstrating, while Bobby sat in a chair, only joining in as they would play through the whole tune. I was immediately impressed at how quickly the Irish kids learned the tune, after hearing it once or twice. I didn't have too much trouble with the jig, but the next tune, the reel 'Lord McDonald', made me sweat . . . I actually remember looking across the room and meeting the Australian guy's eyes, as we both felt somewhat left behind. I was especially puzzled by the bowing across strings which is intrinsic to playing the first part of the reel. I finally asked John Kelly to explain to me what he was doing with the bow. He couldn't really do that in words, so he would just play the same passage again and again, each time bringing his fiddle a little closer under my nose – like someone talking louder to a foreigner . . . Part of the problem was that, being a traditional musician, he was playing that same passage somewhat differently each time, of course, thus adding to my confusion. It was very frustrating, but I kept working on it, and somehow one day (not that week) it clicked.[23]

* * *

The inclusion of set dancing resulted in an explosion of students and prompted some major changes in the organisation of the School, particularly in relation to the choice and availability of suitable venues. From that first dance class in 1982, the dance section has grown to include an unparalleled range of dance-related activities.

The majority of the dances taught at the School are of a type which, until relatively recently, had been rejected by 'authorities', such as An Coimisiún le Rincí Gaelacha (the Commission for Irish Dance), as being either non-Irish, in the case of set dances, or too loosely structured, in the case of the sean-nós. However, the philosophy of the School is to be guided by the cultural practices of the community, rather than the dictates of self-elected authorities.

In the early days, the lack of suitable teachers restricted the range of dances on offer at the School. Eventually, rapidly increasing popularity and the founding of Brook's Academy provided additional support, as Terry Moylan explains:

By 1984 we had established a reasonable reputation for ourselves, to the extent that my wife Kay and I were invited to take another class. Joe had moved to the Community Hall, so we took over Tom Malone's hall [in the centre of Miltown]. We taught alone for a couple of years, until our son was born, and then the situation gradually evolved from my friends in Brook's Academy helping me out to them becoming part of the staff. We ran céilís for the dance students and shared the profits with the School – our share was used to pay the expenses of the Brook's Academy helpers. This has now changed to the School running the céilís and the BA junta being part of the staff.

There were a couple of years before any more teachers were added, and my recollection of who came first is hazy. I always thought that

Connie [Ryan] and Timmy [McCarthy] should have been brought in, and I was glad that Connie was finally invited, if only a year before he died. I think that Paddy Queally and Larry Lynch were among the very early additions, followed by Pat Moroney and Martin Byrnes – not absolutely sure though![24]

In 1989, classes were still restricted to 'Beginners and Polka', 'Caledonian and Mazurka', and 'Plain Set and Lancers', and venues confined to the immediate environs of the town. The traditional Sunday night *céilí* had been reinforced by a programme of 'special *céilis*' on Monday, Tuesday and Thursday nights, again run by Brook's Academy. But the coupling of the School and set dancing was a marriage made in heaven, and, as dancers poured in to Miltown, student numbers rocketed: between 1982 and 1985 they were doubled, and by the 1990s, dancers made up the largest individual group at the School.

The introduction of set dancing classes has posed significant accommodation problems for the School's organisers. Unlike fiddle, pipe, whistle or concertina students, a couple of dozen dancers cannot be easily shuffled into the parlour or kitchen of a house. Dancers need space, and lots of dancers need lots of space! As a result, venues for the School have had to be extended way beyond the bounds of Miltown, with dance classes held in venues such as the Golf Club, GAA Club, Mill Theatre, as well as St Joseph's Secondary School, Spanish Point, and the Quilty Tavern.

The 'traditional' opening *céilí* has now been replaced by an extensive programme of official *céilíthe* in Miltown, Quilty and Spanish Point, each drawing many hundreds of eager participants, as well as providing much work for the once maligned *céilí* bands. During the 2002 event, twenty-four official *céilíthe* were held, with a number of 'unofficial' events available in nearby commercial venues.

The set dance workshop programme for 2001 illustrates the range and diversity of the dances now being performed:

Auban, Labasheeda reel, Paris and Limerick tumblers at the Community Hall, Miltown;
Erin, square jig and Mezerts at the Golf Club, Spanish Point; and
Borlin polka, Corofin plain, south Kerry polka, Rosscahill and old-style north Kerry at St Joseph's School, Spanish Point.

Those attending the set dance workshops are expected to have mastered the basic steps and will usually have, at least, the Caledonian 'under their belt'. For those who need instruction in the steps and rhythm of the Clare set, Aidan Vaughan and Betty McCoy are on hand out at the Quilty Tavern. Here, they attempt to teach the intricacies of the steps and rhythm of the Clare set to seventy of eighty dances from Germany, England, Canada, Finland, France, Spain, Japan and all other quarters of the world. As Aidan commented:

> I always start with the basic reel step, because if you don't have that step, you're wasting your time. Like I say to the class, it's like learning your ABC before learning to read and write, like learning to crawl before you start to walk, or learning your scales before you start your music. No matter how advanced they think they are, I start with the basic step and build up after that, build on the step . . . I have them in a circle with the music slowed down to half-speed, so they can practise the steps – advance and retire, do the steps in place. I get them to do it in a couple – a lady and a gent – then, after a while, I put them into sets of four and do the Caledonian with them.
>
> We start with a basic step and work up. First day, I'll do a simple step, second day, the rhythm . . . five or six or more steps, I add a little bit on to a step, so we progress. I do a little jig step as well for the jig in the Caledonian. There's a nice little treble step. For the hornpipe, I do a similar step to the reel. Some of the older dancers had great steps for the hornpipe, because they probably did a bit of step dancing and they could incorporate steps into the hornpipe [figure]. I know there's an old tradition that women never battered, but you take the women away from set dancing now, you'd have to say good-bye to it – you have to have equality now anyway! So, I teach the women the same as the men, because the majority in my class would be women, anyway.[25]

In St Joseph's GAA Club, Miltown, there are beginners, intermediate and advanced classes in old style step dancing, while in the Mill Theatre on the Ballard Road, Miltown, the intricacies of *sean-nós* (old-style) dancing are demonstrated by Mick Mulkerrins and Mairéad Casey. *Sean-nós* dancing is a distinctive regional style that has survived into the present day, largely in the Connemara Gaeltacht. In appearance, it differs from other styles in encouraging dancers to make much more use of the body and arms. According to accounts of dancing in the nineteenth century, vigorous arm movements were an integral part of the male dance. It is also characterised by a more flat-footed position than other styles and a movement where the dancer uses the heel and the ball of the foot in a rapid rhythmical movement. Not surprisingly, Mick and Mairéad's class is always extremely lively.

For those who wish to see demonstrations from a wide range of the Irish dance tradition, Joe and Siobhan O'Donovan present 'An Evening of Old Style Step and Traditional Set Dancing' on Thursday nights at the Community Hall. Needless to say, this is one recital that is always well attended.

The quality of dance teaching at the School is exceptional – hardly surprising since the teaching staff is a veritable *Who's Who* of the world of traditional dance. In addition to those named, teachers include Pádraig O'Dea, Jerry O'Reilly, Irene Martin, Mary Friel, Eileen O'Doherty, Larry Lynch, Celine and Michael Tubridy, Margaret Wrey, Paddy Neylon, Geraldine Connolly, Mary Clancy, Paddy and Carolyn Hanafin, Joe McGuiggan and Terry Cullen.

The dancing programme might be called the social heart of the School and perhaps best represents the old traditions of music and dance. Although the CD player has replaced the fiddle or the flute, the methods used to teach dancing appear to be timeless, and apart from the comparative luxury of the surroundings, there is little that the dancing masters of old would find strange in the classes of Miltown 2002.

The feet of Pádraig O'Dea (foreground) and his students during his sean-nós *step dancing class,* 2002.

Celine Tubridy demonstrating sean-nós *steps*, 2002.

Unlike the instrumental classes, there is no real attempt to grade students, who are generally expected to select the class that is appropriate for their level of expertise. In the event, it is hardly surprising that some students – perhaps overeager to acquire yet another prize in their personal dance collection – over-estimate their abilities. Although this can result in difficulties for the hard-pressed teachers, problems are usually dismissed with a smile, which typifies the atmosphere of good humour that pervades the occasion.

Notes to Chapter 4

1   For a discussion of music and education in Ireland, see Richard Pine, ed., *Music in Ireland 1848–1998* (Cork: Mercier, 1998); and Marie McCarthy, *Passing It On* (Cork: Cork University Press, 1999).
2   Harry Hughes and Muiris Ó Rócháin, eds., 'From John Joe Lynch to Jimmy Ward: The Musical Heritage of Kilfenora', *Dal gCais*, vol. 4 (1978), p. 91.
3   Quoted in Marie McCarthy, *Passing It On*, p. 39.
4   Junior Crehan, 'Thady Casey, Dancing Master', *Ceol Tire*, no. 9 (1977), pp. 10–11.
5   For further details of the *eisteddfod*, see Prys Morgan, 'From a Death to a View: The Hunt for the Welsh Past in the Romantic Period', in Eric Hobsbawm and Terence Ranger, *The Invention of Tradition* (Cambridge: Cambridge University Press, 1992), p. 43.
6   Quoted in Marie McCarthy, *Passing It On*, p. 75.
7   Joe O'Donovan, 'Evolution and Innovation in Our Hundred Years of Irish Traditional Dancing', in *Crosbhealach an Cheoil*, p. 158.
8   Information taken from official CCÉ website, 'About CCÉ' (www.comhaltas.com), 2 February 2001.
9   Harry Hughes and Muiris Ó Rócháin, 'Willie Clancy: The Man and His Music', *Dal gCais*, vol. 2 (1975), p. 116.
10 Information from official CCÉ website, 2 February 2001.
11 See Hughes and Ó Rócháin, 'Willie Clancy: The Man and His Music', p. 116.
12 From unrecorded statement during fiddle classes at the School, 1975, remembered by the author.
13 Martin Talty, 'Scoil Eigse Willie Clancy', *Dal gCais*, vol. 2 (1975), pp. 83–84.
14 E-mail to Barry Taylor, 19 July 2001.
15 Muiris Ó Rócháin to Barry Taylor.
16 15 Henrietta Street, Dublin 1. This building was acquired in derelict condition and subsequently restored by NPU.
17 Correspondence from Thomas Johnson to Barry Taylor, 2000.
18 Quoted from unpublished correspondence with the author, 2000.
19 Recorded interview with Brendan McGlinchey by Harry Hughes, August 1995.
20 Barry Taylor, 'A Contrast in Styles', *Dal gCais*, vol. 4 (1978), p. 98; this is an abridged version of the author's unpublished dissertation: *Traditional Fiddle Playing in West Clare: Junior Crehan and Michael Downes* (University of Leeds, 1977).
21 Barry Taylor, 'The Fiddler from Kilfarboy', *Dal gCais*, vol. 8 (1986), pp. 48–49.
22 E-mail correspondence from Michael Arden to Barry Taylor, 20 October 2000.
23 E-mail correspondence from Phillippe Varlet to Barry Taylor, 21 October 2000.
24 E-mail correspondence from Terry Moylan to Barry Taylor, 22 November 2001.
25 Recorded conversation between Aidan Vaughen and Barry Taylor, Ballymackea, Mullagh, County Clare, 20 November 2001.

Friday

B Y NOW, THE set dancers in the Community Hall have mastered three of the four new dances that they will learn during the week. This morning, they are tackling another of the sets rescued from oblivion by Dan Furey and James Keane. Teacher Eileen O'Doherty from County Cork is taking participants through yet another complex set of figures. As the dozen sets whirl into action, teacher Gerry O'Reilly receives a crack across the head as his charges fail to execute a complicated manoeuvre correctly. Gerry smiles and pretends to defend himself against further attack.

* * *

Just across the street from the Community Hall stands Kate O'Loughlin's house. Brid O'Donohue's thirteen whistle students must make their way through Kate's kitchen and out into the backyard, where the class is held in a small brick outbuilding. This morning, Brid announces that they will take their chairs outside as the early morning rain has given way to bright sunshine. This is a fairly large and very mixed group, although, unlike many of the other classes, all the students are Irish, with half a dozen local youngsters combining with adult students from all parts of the country – North and South. The significant age differences between the students doesn't seem to adversely affect matters.

'Let's try that jig – "Deva the Dancer" – and I'll show you a variation to finish the turn.' Only when she is satisfied that each student has mastered the jig, Brid returns to a march that had been started earlier. 'I'll play the first part through again, then we'll move on to the second part.' Like many of the other teachers, Brid favours breaking the tune into phrases and refuses to

Eileen O'Doherty and James Keane during an evening céilí, *1994.*

Paul Raffo (foreground) and fellow students, Brid O'Donoghue's whistle class, 1999.

move on to a new phrase until she is happy that each student has it. 'Try to put a cut on the G,' she advises. 'You can tell it's a march by the way everyone's feet go "dum-dum" at the end of the first part. You can imagine that you're playing in a marching band – dum-dum.' Eamon from Belfast is having a problem with the rhythm, and Brid explains that it's because he's putting an extra F in the last phrase. Young Finbar sitting next to him has caught the habit but manages to correct himself.

Brid asks whether any of the class play other instruments, and a forest of arms shoot up, with fiddle, concertina, bodhran and even the harp getting a mention. She tells the class: 'For the final part of Saturday morning, we'll have an impromptu session. If you want to bring other instruments, you're quite welcome.' Then it's back to the work of the week, and the group launch into a tune learned earlier. This time, it's the set dance, 'The Three Sea Captains'. Brid suggests putting two hornpipes together, 'Poll Halfpenny' and 'Mrs Galvin's'. Halfway through the second tune, Brid asks the class to stop playing. 'This is one of those tunes that's played only once through. OK, now let's try "Dark is the Colour". You know, it's very difficult for a group of people to play an air together, but take it really slowly and watch my fingers carefully.'

Even from thirteen whistles in near unison, Brid is able to detect that a couple of her students are playing a high G when it should be a G in the low register. As in all other cases, the error is pointed out in the most kindly and considerate manner, and the attitude of the students confirms their complete respect for their teacher. 'Now I mentioned "Kitty's Gone a-Milking" – this was one of Willie Clancy's favourite tunes. You remember what I said earlier about short and long rolls? You need a good long G roll in the first phrase or you'll lose time.' Halfway round the circle, Brid points out to Maisie that her rolls would be more effective using other fingers. 'You have it right, but if you use your other fingers, you can get a better effect with less effort.'

* * *

Besides posing a technical challenge, the flute presents a physical challenge, demanding good posture and a mastery of breathing in order to achieve the correct tonal output. Not surprisingly, technical issues are high on the agenda in Marcas Ó Murchú's flute class. The class is asked to play a couple of jigs learned earlier, and Marcas walks around checking individual tone production and carefully adjusting the posture of individuals and the position of the instrument where necessary. But this class is not simply about technique, and Marcas spends a lot time discussing the background to the tunes and individual players.

'Can anyone remember what we said about keeping the tradition alive?' One teenager responds, 'Remembering what went before!'

'Good lad,' says Marcas. 'Now let's see if anyone can play one of the tunes that we learned yesterday.' Fergus volunteers with a superb rendering of a reel. 'Do you know,' says Marcas, 'Fergus' mother told me that he was up at 7.30 this morning practising that tune – even before he had breakfast.

'Now, we're going to learn a new reel. Have a listen to this one.' Marcas tells the class that they have been listening to Phillip Duffy. 'The tune was composed by a great fiddle player from Sligo called Martin Wynne and is usually called "Martin Wynne's Number One". I am going to play the recording through again, and I want you to listen carefully and try to hum along with it.' After several times through, many of the group are able to hum the tune. 'After the break, we'll have a go at playing it – but it's a fiddle tune, so can anyone see a problem that it might present?' A student from Ohio suggests that flute players will have problem managing the notes below D – the lowest note on the concert flute. Marcas agrees. 'That's a common problem for flute players, so we'll try to find some solutions.'

Marcas O Murchú (centre) and his class, 2002.

Marcas Ó Murchú correcting a student's posture, 1999.

Chapter 5

A Touchstone for the Tradition?

DURING THE WEEK of the School, some 5,000 people pack into Miltown each day to enjoy the ambience created by the hundreds of musicians, singers and dancers involved in the School. Although the countless sessions taking place give the event a festive flavour, it must again be stressed that: 'The Willie Clancy Summer School is an educational institution. It promotes the study and practice of Irish traditional music, song and dance.'[1]

From the eighty students of 1973, enrolments rose to the low hundreds by the end of the decade and reached four figure totals by the mid-1990s. Curiously, in 1997, the organisers thought that enrolments had peaked as numbers fell to around 900. The following year, however, the attendance shot up by around 30 per cent to a total of 1,250, with big increases for all instruments, particularly the fiddle and the pipes. In the years since, enrolments have continued to grow, with the total of full- and part-time students approaching 1,500 in 2001, doubtless fuelled by the continued global explosion of interest in Irish music.[2]

Such a performance would be staggering for a professional organisation. However, although the School is now considered to be one of Irish music's major events, it is still largely an amateur affair, run by enthusiasts for enthusiasts. There has never been a serious attempt at sales or marketing, and advertising has been kept to an absolute minimum. The organisers do not issue glossy brochures, and following the pattern established by the typed offerings of the first two years, its printed programmes remain little more than a daily listing of activities.

The School's publicity is largely conducted on a word-of-mouth basis. From the first year, most students came as a result of personal recommendation, and, to this day, that is the way that most people learn about the School.[3]

The high number of students who attend on the personal recommendation of former students is one indication of the School's qualitative success, as is the large percentage of students who make return visits. The School's organisers do not carry out any regular detailed analysis of attendance figures, but in a one-off analysis in 1995, repeat enrolments were estimated at around 40 per cent. However, an independent survey suggested the figure could be as high as 70 per cent, which, in the terminology of management, demonstrates a remarkable degree of customer satisfaction.[4] This is also indicated by the extremely low rate of complaints received about teaching matters. These generally tend to originate from parents dissatisfied with the lack of individual tuition received by their children or the placing of their children in inappropriate classes (usually perceived to be of too low a standard).

Occasionally, comment is received on the size of classes. However, to a great extent, the growth in class sizes, particularly for popular instruments

Fiddle Students, 2002.

such as the fiddle, is an unavoidable consequence of the growing success of the School and the concomitant difficulty of finding sufficient suitable teachers and venues. Some people have requested that classes be extended to cover instruments such as the banjo, bodhran, bazouki and guitar. Putting aside any value judgement on the acceptability of such instruments in the School's core philosophy, the lack of additional accommodation is likely to limit any further expansion.

Due to the School's determination to avoid artificially devised standards, such as those demanded in competitive playing or concert performance, the School does not place any demands on students to achieve predetermined objectives. Consequently, there are no formal assessment processes, nor do students receive any formal recognition of their performance. Generally, the only performance standards are those set by the participants for themselves. Teachers such as Martin Hayes encourage their students to set some personal aims for the week. However, even where this technique is practised, there is no systematic evaluation of results. In fact, the only time that any form of assessment is carried out is in the enrolment process.

Following their observations of the young people who had flocked to Miltown to learn from Willie Clancy, the School's organisers wanted to create a situation where young enthusiasts could meet with the musicians, singers and dancers of the older generation. In the early years of the School, the relatively small numbers permitted a more informal relationship between students and teachers, although the structured nature of the event certainly introduced a degree of formality. However, the structure was always intended to keep it to a minimum. The basic framework of the School has remained largely unchanged over three decades, but the individual events that make up that programme – and particularly the classes, which are at the heart of proceedings – are largely under the control of the individual teachers and are conducted in an extremely relaxed and informal manner.

In this and many other ways, the School cannot be easily compared with more familiar systems of education. In more recent times, much of the teaching of traditional music has been controlled by CCÉ. Although many individuals within CCÉ, particularly at branch level, still follow their own teaching programmes and methods, CCÉ has emulated formal education in encouraging their teachers to implement set systems of teaching, and in student performance and assessment. A strong emphasis is placed on preparing students for competitions and concert playing, including processes that can be compared to the 'grinds' used by the students of mainstream academic subjects to prepare for examinations. CCÉ now offers a teaching

Former student, Joe Toolan from Dublin, teaching fiddle, 1999.

Tommy McCarthy with a young concertina student, 1992.

diploma based on an annual course at the *Cultúrlann* (CCÉ headquarters in Dublin), and to date over 400 teachers have gained this qualification.[5]

To some extent, this development has both foreshadowed and responded to the social and economic changes that have overtaken Irish music in recent years. As memories of the *clachan* have receded and the community of traditional musicians, dancers and singers has gradually shifted from the western fringes of Ireland to its urban centres and, latterly, to encompass a global community, the provision of music teaching has assumed an ever more commercial profile. The increasing numbers of competent musicians emerging from CCÉ's mass teaching programmes find it hard to make a living as performers, and teaching is seen as an alternative.

In comparison, the School offers no financial incentives to its teachers, depending instead on their dedication to maintaining and passing on a shared philosophy of the tradition. Roughly, this translates to a belief that traditional culture is not an object for individual commercial exploitation, but a possession to be shared by a community. On its part, the School does not impose either a rigid curriculum or an over-arching system of standards on its teaching 'staff', but relies on their individual ability to pass on the shared philosophy.

This has been possible partly because of the long-term participation of a fairly sizeable number of musicians, singers and dancers and enhanced

The extended Crehan family playing at the Ceol Choirm Mór (Grand Concert), *1993. Left to right: Angela (Crotty), Mick, Ita, Niall, Kieran, Junior, Kevin, Eric Rigler (guest musician), P. J. Crotty and Tony.*

by the involvement of families, often over several generations. Notable among these are the Kelly (now with three generations involved in teaching), O'Connor, Peoples, McCarthy, McPeake, Hayes, McKeon, Glackin, Crehan and Potts families. Linked into these family groupings are their long-time musical associates. Many of these have acquired their knowledge of Irish traditional music as a result of this association and have assumed the status of 'musical in-laws'.

The School has now developed several generations of teachers, including a substantial corps who have 'graduated' through its ranks. Although if asked, most if not all of the School's teaching staff would sign on to the overall philosophy of the School's founders, factors such as family background, location, age group, technical skill, musical knowledge and playing experience will each play a part in determining individual interpretation.

Commenting on the development of this philosophy, Nicholas Carolan, director of the Irish Traditional Music Archive and an active supporter and participant in the School, observed:

> Another attractive feature of the School is that they've almost recreated a kind of traditional society. With its fragmentation, people in urban life have become individuals, or individual family units, separated units . . . [At the School people] pay their dues by attending, talking, by playing, by interacting socially, year after year after year . . . There's some core existence there that has been retained . . .[6]

There is no doubt that the broad community of the School is of a very different type from the tightly knit community of the *clachan*. One area where significant change can be observed is in the practice of unaccompanied singing. Before it was possible to simply switch on the radio, people sought relief from the boredom of repetitive tasks by singing. The great Connemara singer Darach Ó Catháin described lying in bed listening to his mother sing and the way that visitors to the house would often exchange a song or two with the occupants.[7] Singing was an integral part of both the informal *cuaird* or more formal social gatherings, often whilst the dancers were resting or the musicians were taking some much needed refreshment. Although the custom of singing remained largely unaltered during the *clachan* period, new songs were adopted into the traditional repertoire – a practice that even managed to survive the change in everyday language from Irish to English. However, as with dancing, the move from kitchen to public house wrought significant changes. Many singers who were happy to sing in the quiet of the home found the experience of singing to an audience of strangers daunting. The noise level of modern lounge bars also provided a challenge to solo singing that few could meet, and thus the ballad group was born. Although ballad groups drew upon the traditional repertoire to a great part, their singing styles, usually based on exploiting the benefits of amplification, drew more on popular and classical techniques than the *sean-nós*.

In the earlier days of the School, singing in the traditional fashion played a much more significant part, particularly in the unofficial activities. Although formal lectures on both English and Irish-language song and an afternoon singing recital have always formed an important part of the programme, and the traditional singing workshop has been added, there seems to be less of a welcome for an unaccompanied song in the informal pub sessions. Even the singing session that generally takes place in Marrinan's bar at lunchtime seems to provide evidence of the increasing ghettoisation of traditional singing.

* * *

In general, any exploration and analysis of Irish music is bedevilled by the scarcity of accurate information on its practice even up to fairly recent times. The information deficit has, historically, had a profound effect on the teaching and performance of Irish traditional music, promoting the development of a whole catalogue of innovative and, sometimes, spurious methods and standards.

At its most basic, any musician or dancer needs two things: a repertoire of dances and/or tunes and the technical skills required for their performance. What sets apart the 'classical' and the 'traditional' musician is largely the context in which the repertoire is both learned and performed. The School's founding objective was to enable the musical culture of the local community to be passed on to future generations by its practitioners, thus, hopefully, maintaining its 'traditional' context. Given that the community that provided the context has disappeared and that the School has no set curriculum, the responsibility for providing the context is placed almost entirely on the teachers. Apart from variations in individual teaching skills, the major identifiable difference in approach appears to be the relative importance ascribed to the three elements of technique, repertoire and information on the context. (The latter is generally referred to in educational circles as 'underpinning knowledge'.)

In the classes where students are assumed to have limited technical skills, such as some piping and dancing classes, the balance of time will be used to develop the technical ability of the student. Conversely, in the classes

Phil Callery, 1994.

where students are assumed to have highly developed skills, more time is likely to be spent on repertoire building and discussing context – the class of Martin Hayes described in the diary provides a good example of the latter. In between lie a large number of 'mixed ability' classes such as that of Marcas Ó Múrchú, where teachers attempt to balance the three elements.

Thus, although the basic methodology is common, the implementation is as varied as the backgrounds of the individual teachers involved. Although the teachers working at the School are not required to undergo any pre-training or assessment, as it happens, a number are professional teachers, although generally not in the discipline of music. Some members of the staff, particularly the younger teachers, have become music teachers in order to 'exploit' their musical skills. However, many of those are not in the formal education system and have not undergone any formal teacher training.

In addition to the absence of formal curricula, there is little or no guidance provided by the School on the use of teaching aids. Although this might at first glance seem a rather peripheral point, the use of one teaching

Tommy McCarthy with granddaughters Annie Ruth Benagh and Siobhán Keane, 1994.

aid in traditional music teaching has had a profound effect on the development of the music over the last fifty years: musical notation.

Discussing the use of notation, Breandán Breathnach sought to show extensive use in both the transmission and teaching of traditional music.[8] With regards to transmission, he divides the process into two categories: the works produced 'in order to preserve some part of the national heritage for posterity', which include those of academic collectors such as Bunting, Petrie and Joyce, which were 'directed to a literate public, who, like themselves, were outside the tradition'; and those initiated by individuals who 'were themselves performers and whose collections were directed to learners and fellow practitioners'. In this category, Breathnach mentions only the various works of Francis O'Neill of Chicago (published in the early years of the twentieth century)[9] and Pat Mitchell's praiseworthy *The Dance Music of Willie Clancy* (published in 1976). In fact, the bibliography of tune books in Vallely's *Companion to Irish Music* suggests that there was precious little else published in the years separating these publications.

Up to the 1950s, there seem to be few published records of any systematic use of musical notation in the teaching of traditional music. However,

A student in Máire O'Keefe's class writes down 'Andy Dixon's Reel', 1992.

there is some evidence of traditional musicians gaining their initial musical training in brass, military or flute bands, in which the use of staff notation would have been normal, and of a few teachers of traditional music using notation in their teaching, including non-conventional forms, which generally attempt to replicate the fingering used on a particular instrument.

Although Breathnach recognised the historic role played by printed music in the preservation and transmission of Irish traditional music, he had firm views on its limitations for the transmission of traditional style: '. . . staff notation does not reflect the ordinary differences in duration which exist between these visually equal quavers, much less display those subtle deviations which give life and colour to the performance of a good player. Only by constant listening can this rhythmic quality be attained.'[10]

Breathnach believed that the use of notation for an instrumentalist might be equated to the way that a traditional singer might use a printed

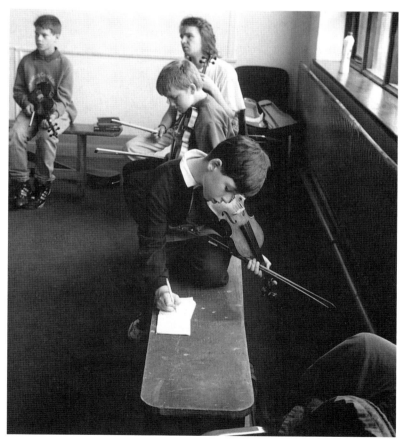

A young student in Dermy Diamond's class writing down a new tune, 1994.

song text: simply a way of acquiring the basic information. He concluded that, ultimately, the style of the player depends more on the way that the player first acquired his or her music than how individual items in his or her repertoire are learned. Thus 'to play as to the manner born one must learn by ear rather than by eye, as we all have done in learning our first language'.

In the Irish dance tradition, music for dance forms such as the quadrille-based set was bound within a strict set of conventions. These included set rhythmic patterns (jig-time, reel-time, polka-time, etc.), set time frames (so many bars for each figure of the dance) and set practices, depending on local variations of the dance. All these conventions were learned within the community and were shared by musicians and dancers alike. Although printed collections might be used to supplement tunes learned aurally, the learner was expected to rely on the aural tradition to acquire phrasing, rhythm and ornamentation.

Contemporary practice in the School suggests that some form of notation is present in around 50 per cent of the instrumental classes, with,

John Kelly, Jr (right) and student, 1999. John is the third generation of the Kelly family to teach fiddle at the School.

perhaps, its use most prevalent in the fiddle classes. It appears that many of the younger students who come to the School are extremely dependent on musical notation – increasingly, it seems, conventional staff notation. Perhaps not surprisingly, its use as a teaching aid seems more prevalent in the younger generation of teachers.

Although recordings reproduce a specific performance frozen in time, the medium is able to capture many of the subtle nuances of the performance: 'those subtle deviations that give life and colour to the performance of a good player'. Although some players reproduce recordings note-for-note (and they are free to do so if this is what they desire), the majority use them either to boost their own repertoires or to improve their technical skills. In the process, they often introduce subtle variations into the originals.

The use of notation reduces the ability of the musician to internalise his or her repertoire. Thus, its use poses a numer of potential consequences for the future of Irish traditional music. The first, as Breathnach suggested, is likely to be a reduction in the communal national repertoire of traditional music: that is, the combined repertoires of all the individual players. A reliance solely on noted melodies and their variants means that those not transcribed will not be played and will be lost. Secondly, one of the major creative dynamics of the oral/aural tradition – the process of individual vari-ation and creativity – will gradually decline. This is the process that produced all the individual tune variants (some so varied as to form new tunes) that have been introduced into the repertoire. Thirdly, the wide variations in style that have been previously observable from parish to parish will be quickly wiped out, if players come to rely on standard noted versions of tunes.

Breathnach pointed to a situation in Scotland where, over the last two centuries, 'folk and art music have fused', with the tone and technique of the art musician being applied to traditional forms. In recent years, the global spread of Irish music has encouraged its take-up and practice by many trained musicians, particularly classically trained violin players. The recent use of Irish music in many different musical forms – from its use by Shaun Davey in symphonic music to the offerings of Sharon Shannon and her musical colleagues in the realm of contemporary popular music – suggests that Breathnach's predictions of 1985 have long come to pass.

Every generation and community probably had performers who, by their sheer artistry and creativity, could cause an assembly to stop and listen. In the area around Miltown, fiddle players Bobby Casey and Junior Crehan and, of course, Willie Clancy were noteworthy solo performers, as well as solid dance musicians. However, the soloists were always outnumbered by the great army of general 'dance music practitioners', who provided the

Tommy Peoples (left) and James Kelly, 1999.

Yvonne Griffin plays a new tune as her students copy it down from the blackboard, 1998.

music's dynamic force and were largely responsible for the development of the myriad of local styles, techniques and repertoires. Not surprisingly, the most noticeable characteristic of this music was its rhythmical quality, and any individual creativity was always balanced by the need to maintain a solid rhythm. As Jimmy Ward said, 'In my youth, you were strictly judged by the way in which you played for the set. Nothing else mattered. . .'

However, as the function of the music has changed, and music for dancing has been largely replaced by music to entertain a passive audience, it is the player's technical skill that is, increasingly, admired – as with concert musicians. As a result, the limelight has been firmly focussed on those musicians with well-developed performance techniques, with improvisation, ornamentation and innovation to the fore. In one well-documented case, a fiddle player with an impeccable 'traditional' background but with a style that totally precludes its use for dancing has been hailed as signalling the way forward for traditional dance music.[11]

In the early days of commercial recording, good dance musicians were required to meet the demands of an audience familiar with dance music, and the resulting records were often used to provide the music for dancing. Recording methods were basic. Musicians played a selection of dance tunes into a microphone until a red light signalled that the recording was due to stop. The conventions of the record industry demanded accompaniment, and this was invariably provided by the recording company's in-house pianist. The results were patchy to say the least, as many of the greatest names in Irish music struggled to overcome accompanists who had little or no knowledge of the structure of the music.

This is in strong contrast to today's productions, which are carefully tailored to meet the demands of a general audience, many of whom are unfamiliar with the structure and form of traditional dance music. Production usually involves lengthy planning, careful arrangements and the use of a variety of instruments hitherto considered non-traditional for the addition of various layers of accompaniment. (Recent CD releases of Irish 'traditional' music have included the Greek bazouki, cello, viola, harp, mandocello and synthesiser.) Such offerings necessitate the development of a much wider range of skills by its practitioners, whose techniques have, increasingly, come to resemble those of the classically trained musician. It is, therefore, hardly surprisingly that recent recorded Irish music has involved classical and jazz musicians.

One effect of the set dancing revival has been the resurgence of the *céilí* band. *Céilí* band musicians – many of whom either teach at the School or have passed through as students – are no longer the reviled pariahs of Irish

Joe Ryan, from Inagh, west Clare, playing in a session in the Central Hotel, Miltown Malbay, in 1993. Joe was the honoured subject of a tribute by fellow musicians and admirers during the 2002 School.

music, and traditional music outlets now abound with audio cassettes and CDs of tunes specially compiled and recorded by *céilí* bands for dancers. However, the rapprochement between musicians and dancers has not been fully achieved at the School. In spite of the presence of large numbers of 'dance musicians', it is rare to see dancing practised outside the classes other than at the School's programme of *céilíthe*. In these, the music is provided by *céilí* bands specifically engaged for the occasion.

Some of the musicians attending the School appear to wish to avoid playing for dancing at all costs! However, it is equally true that many revival dancers demand a very high standard of performance to accompany their own, often modest, efforts. Bearing this in mind, it would certainly help musicians with little or no experience in playing for dancing to have some suitable opportunity to gain this experience. Perhaps some thought might

Jimmy O'Brien Moran, from Tramore, County Waterford, plays at one of the daily lunchtime recitals organised by Na Píobairí Uilleann, 1999.

be given to arranging situations where inexperienced musicians might be 'schooled' in the art of dance playing, and, equally, some dancers whose terpsichorean skills have been honed to the cassette player and compact disc might benefit from some live assistance.

* * *

In addition to the effect of the School on the individual, it has been a catalyst for the development of traditional music studies in Ireland. In 1987, the editor of An Píobaire commented:

> The popularity of traditional music has resulted in large numbers wishing to attend the Willie Clancy Summer School and the effect has been to make the music even more popular by raising standards through expert and effective tuition in the classes. Thus, the effects affect and increase the demand for succeeding years, ensuring continuity and constantly increasing expertise in all areas. The greatest tribute is that others should follow where initiators have lead and this year, 1987, sees other teaching summer schools – at Tubbercurry in Sligo and Glencolmcille in Donegal. There has also been a proliferation of mini-summer schools, long weekends of activity. To the newer schools, we send our best wishes for their success this year and in the future. To our old friends in Miltown Malbay, we can only wish continued success for many years to come.[12]

If imitation is, truly, the sincerest form of flattery, the School's organisers should be highly flattered as, since 1987, commemorative music festivals and schools have proliferated throughout Ireland. In Clare alone we can find festivals of music, song or dance in Feakle, Kilrush, Tulla, Ennistymon, Doonbeg and Labasheeda, with many more held throughout the country. Generally, these events are based around class-based teaching sessions, but they also include formal recitals, concerts and, of course, the usual plethora of informal pub sessions. However, in recent years there has been an increasing tendency to include more academic activities, such as lectures and workshops. In all cases, it is hard to escape the effect of the Willie Clancy Summer School on such events.

Turning to the formal education sector, since 1998 traditional music has become an option at GCSE level in Northern Ireland, and at both junior and leaving certificate level in the Republic, although as late as 1999 there was no formal teacher training in the subject available in either country. In fact, as late as 1997 only 25 per cent of the Republic's 759 second-level schools included music in the curriculum. At first-level (national) schools, perhaps more encouragingly, many schools now offer opportunities for pupils to learn traditional music and dance, although classes are generally available outside the formal curriculum.

Inevitably, any analysis of the effect of the School on traditional music education in Ireland must involve a consideration of the role of CCÉ as the major provider of music and dance teaching (there is virtually no organised teaching of traditional song in Ireland) over the last fifty years.[13] Up to recent times, CCÉ's teaching programme was largely outside the formal arena, with most teaching performed on an ad-hoc basis, although generally coordinated through its branches. Whether the concept of a 'national' summer school, which had been mooted in the early 1970s, would have reached fruition without the initiative of the Willie Clancy Memorial Committee and the subsequent launch of the School is open to speculation. However, following CCÉ's withdrawal after the first year of the School, an annual summer school or *Scoil Éigse* was launched, and this has now become an annual CCÉ event held in late August in conjunction with the *Fleadh Cheoil na hÉireann*. Ironically, at branch level, many CCÉ teachers recommend their students to attend the Willie Clancy Summer School in order to absorb the 'real tradition'.

At third level, before the 1990s, opportunities for the academic study of traditional music, song and dance were extremely limited. Prior to the establishment of the School, the main opportunity to study Irish music was in the course on traditional music provided as part of the bachelor of music degree course at University College, Cork. Although a number of institutions now offer some tuition in traditional music, the most significant advances in third-level education have been achieved at the University of Limerick (founded 1989), through the establishment of its Irish World Music Centre (IWMC). Under the direction of Professor Mícheál Ó Súilleabáin, a long-time regular contributor to the School, the IWMC offers a comprehensive programme of graduate and post-graduate courses in all the disciplines associated with traditional music, song and dance.

It is difficult to assess the influence of the School on the founding and development of either the IWMC or in activities in any other part of the Irish education system. Perhaps the least that can be said is that it has stimulated an interest in traditional music for tens of thousands of young people over the last three decades. In addition, the publicity for the IWMC's own summer school (*Blas*) confirms more than a passing acquaintance with the methods employed by the Willie Clancy Summer School.

The School's growth has meant that it now affects most of the towns and villages within a radius of at least ten miles around Milltown. During the week of the School, the town itself bursts into life. The main street echoes with a plethora of dialects and languages, its many bars are crammed to bursting point, and the sounds of jigs, reels and hornpipes fill the air. However, assessing the impact that the School has had on the area presents some problems.

It should be realised that an invasion of holidaymakers is not an entirely new phenomenon. The near proximity of the popular beaches at Spanish Point and White Strand had brought visitors in the summer months for many decades before the launch of the School. This trade in tourism was bolstered from the 1950s by the launch of the Spanish Point Holiday Festival, which like the more famous Rose of Tralee focused on a female beauty

Willie Keane, late of Doonbeg, County Clare, 1994. A noted local dancer, Willie was a regular teacher at the School.

A street session featuring Brian McNamara (top with pipes), one of the School's piping teachers, 2001.

pageant, known as the Darlin' Girl from Clare. Like the Rose, the Darlin' Girl was a title inspired by a popular song, which had no known connection to the west Clare resort. The Darlin' Girl was a strictly commercial affair and originated in an initiative launched by Ireland's fledgling tourist board, *An Bord Fáilte* (literally, the Welcome Board), to promote Irish tourism – a concept known as *An Tostal*, the pageant.

The decade of the 1990s was a period of intense economic activity in Ireland, which prompted investment in some of Miltown's infrastructure. Although the School has brought significant material benefits to its host town, the last three decades have also witnessed a general modernisation of Ireland, making it difficult to accurately quantify the material contribution made by the School to the town.

Harry Hughes arrived in Miltown in the late sixties and is in a good position to assess the impact of both the School and the economic upturn of 1990s:

> The improvement of facilities in Miltown Malbay itself – the improvement of shops, the improvement of the decor and the facilities in pubs, general street improvements, painting – I think that has a direct relationship to the income from the Willie Clancy. In other words, this is extra earned income that has been ploughed back, resources that have been ploughed back into the buildings, into the physical fabric, into the extension, into the development. . . [but] you now have this phenomenon called the Celtic Tiger which means that there's cheap money available and the economy booming in general, and, obviously, this is having a knock-on effect, too.[14]

In the earlier years of the School, visitors – a high percentage of whom enrolled as students – tended to come individually or in small groups. Many of the visitors were young and looking for self-catering budget accommodation, such as camp or caravan sites. However, as time has passed and visitors have arrived in ever-increasing numbers, the trend has been towards family groups. Their demand for improved accommodation has been answered by a massive growth in guesthouses, restaurants and hotels.

The income that has flowed into the town has also meant that the facilities available in pubs have improved considerably since the editor of *Na Píobaire* was moved to comment adversely on facilities in 1976: a definite plus-point for visitors. Fortunately, such changes appear to have had little impact on the School itself. As Finbar Boyle commented:

I don't think that it really has any effect on the School as such, because I think those things are largely peripheral to what goes on during the day. The changes I have seen: at least the pubs have toilets, you can wash yourself in them. I don't like the current trend to make every pub a big pub, and I think that some of the things they did in some of the pubs are not to my liking, but I don't own the pub! I don't think that they affect the core function of the School.[15]

As Harry Hughes points out, the material benefits resulting from the presence of tens of thousands of visitors to Miltown are relatively easy to see. However, the impact of their presence on Miltown's inhabitants, and the relationship between the permanent residents and the School, with its thousands of students and visitors, is much more difficult to assess. To some extent, the importance that music, song and dance play in the life of individual residents will shape their attitudes towards the School. There was some disagreement in local opinion from the outset on the nature of the most fitting memorial to the life of Willie Clancy, and subsequently differences have arisen on the direction that the School should take. Although some of these concern the running of the School, a number concern the relationship between the School and the town.

As a result of the continuing growth of the School, Miltown Malbay assumed the status of 'traditional music capital of Ireland' in the last two decades of the twentieth century. In fact, following the worldwide explosion of interest in Irish music over the last two decades, it might be truly claimed as its *global* capital, although this might be little apparent to someone arriving in Miltown on a cold, wet and windy night in late January.

The proliferation of organised tour groups visiting west Clare from as far afield as the USA and Japan in recent years confirms that some form of cultural tourism is well under way. Commercialism to date has been limited largely to an increase in shops selling artefacts related to traditional music, such as CDs. Away from the week of the School, enhanced interest in music has prompted some publicans to promote regular music sessions – an activity not exclusive to Miltown or west Clare. To date, the music-related interests of visitors to the School, such as sales of musical instruments, have been met largely by outsiders trading in the town during the week.

As yet, there has been no attempt at a Willie Clancy museum, nor is there any evidence of the level of exploitation experienced in, for example, Kentucky's Blue Ridge Mountains, where: 'In the early 1960s, "hillbilly" shows were performed for tourists on the edges of the road. Men in crooked hats and women in long, flowered dresses with holes in them played music and

A street session, 2001.

demonstrated whisky stills and other putative trappings of a culture in dis-
solution. . .'[16]

However, the signs for the future might not be too good if the general
evidence presented elsewhere in Ireland is anything to go by. This suggests
that, unlike many other aspects of the community's heritage, such as the
countryside, national monuments, parks and museums, its musical heritage
is seen largely a means to boost the tourist trade. Thus, it is to be hoped
that, if there is to be any concerted effort at exploiting the musical heritage
of west Clare, it will be kept out of the hands of both the private and state
sectors of the tourist industry.[17]

Finally, when considering the impact of the School on the locality, it
should be noted that since 1973 a sizeable number of people have also cho-
sen to relocate to the area. Many of these have come as a result of either
attending the School or as a result of the ongoing portrayal of the area as a
bastion of traditional culture. Many of the new population are among the
most active in both commercial and voluntary sectors in the area. In addition, newcomers constitute a significant, if not majority, proportion of the
participants in local traditional music activities.[18]

* * *

Although an appeal to the past is among the commonest strategies used to
interpret the present, it is a strategy fraught with danger. Not only is there
the possibility of disagreement about what actually happened in the past
and what the past was, but also the question arises as to whether the past
really is past, or whether it continues, perhaps in different forms.[19] In relation to the status of the School, can it be seen as the heir of past traditions,
is it a revival activity or, at worst, perhaps some kind of invented tradition?[20]

The surges of interest in traditional music, usually away from the areas in
which it was being practised, that have occurred at various times over the
last century or so have often been termed 'revivals'. However, there is little
doubt that traditional music was in a healthy condition in many parts of Ireland at the time of the late nineteenth century 'revival', although it was,
probably, invisible to its largely urban-based evangelists. Likewise, the evidence suggests that the 'tradition' was still flourishing into the mid-1950s,
although it may have largely retreated westerly. Perhaps the state of 'the tradition' might be considered a more contentious question in the period since
the 1960s – a period that witnessed the extinction of the final flickering rem-
nants of country house dance and a continuous migration of both people
and music from the country to the town.

The founding of the School came during a period of renaissance for Ireland's traditional music but while it was still being practised in some of the communities to which it was indigenous. However, until fairly recently, its practice was limited largely to the island of Ireland and those places where the Irish had settled overseas. Today, Irish music is popular worldwide and is promoted through the mainstream channels of the entertainment industry. In recent years, the Internet has enabled easy global communication between enthusiasts of Irish music and has helped the spread of traditional practices that were once restricted to the rural hinterland of Ireland. Countless websites are dedicated to Irish music, song and dance, while aficionados can debate the topic of the day in a number of dedicated cyber forums. In a recent development, it is now possible to learn to play Irish music from the comfort of the home by enrolling with an on-line school, set up and run by some of Ireland's leading practitioners of traditional music.

As the spectrum has broadened, new concepts and practices have been introduced into Irish music. As time has passed and the global spread of Irish music has created new audiences and practitioners, memories have inevitably faded. To many of the new enthusiasts – both national and non-national – the great names of the recent past, such as Willie Clancy, Séamus Ennis, Bobby Casey and Junior Crehan, have undoubtedly lost some of their significance. The new generation of young musicians has created its own idols, as the music assumes roles undreamed of by its earlier progenitors. But should that come as any surprise to us? We know that the great names of the more immediate past also had their idols, with names such as Michael Coleman, Leo Rowsome, Patsy Tuohy and John McKenna springing quickly to mind. In addition, we have seen that they happily and enthusiastically embraced innovations such as the *céilí* band and, later, Seán Ó Riada's *Ceoltóirí Chualann*.

It was this embrace of innovation that provided the starting point for one of the most ambitious and ultimately controversial explorations of Irish music: the television series A *River of Sound*.[21] In this analysis of contemporary practices in Irish traditional music, its writer and presenter, Professor Mícheál Ó Súilleabháin, director of the Irish World Music Centre at the University of Limerick, proposed the notion that, change being a natural concomitant of continuity, innovative practices should be welcomed into the canon of traditional music.

During a TV programme celebrating the launch of the series, the well-known musician and broadcaster Tony McMahon voiced some disquiet on the nature of some of the music introduced by Mícheál Ó Súilleabháin in the programme and purporting to be of the 'tradition'. On the night, McMahon's remarks were met with uproar and shouts of 'begrudger' from the studio audience – an audience, one must say, that contained most of the 'heroic names' of traditional music of the late twentieth century.[22] However, many musicians – particularly those of the older generation – later contacted McMahon to thank him for his comments. The ensuing furore led to one of the more important chapters in the study of Irish music: the Crossroads Conference of 1996 (*Crosbhealach an Cheoil*),[23] which initiated an exploration of the apparent paradox between innovation and tradition. Sadly, the opportunity to develop the Conference into a more structured and regular forum was not taken. Fours years later, the discussion was resumed in a seminar, 'Trends in Traditional Music in the Late Twentieth Century', held at the School, which included many of the main contenders on both sides of the argument. Certainly, the passionate debate that followed the keynote presentations showed that many of the issues raised by A *River of Sound* remain unresolved.

But the School may provide us with more than just a convenient talking shop. The School might be said to bridge the gap between the old and new generations of traditional musicians. Although nowadays not as isolated as in former times, it is located in an area still respected as a preserve of the old musical traditions. With its ethos of self-help and anti-commercialism, the School has a role as a counterpoint to the materialism and individualism that threatens to overtake traditional music, dance and song. It represents a microcosm of the struggle between those who promote individual excellence for the few and those who see the tradition as about participation and cooperation, and its many 'graduates' have each embarked on his or her own unique attempt to balance the past with the present. It might be said that the School stands at the crossroads of custom and innovation.

Assessing the effect that the School has had to date on the practice of Irish music, both in Ireland and overseas, is extremely difficult. At least 20,000 people have received tuition at the classes and probably a similar number have attended organised recitals and lectures. Given that much of the tuition is provided within the context of a shared belief in the importance of the values that underpinned the culture of the *clachans*, it must be assumed that at least some of this philosophy will have been absorbed by the students.

The organisers' records indicate that around 40 per cent of registered students and an unknown, but probably equal, percentage of informal visitors originate from outside the island of Ireland, notably from the United Kingdom, mainland Europe, North America, Japan, Australia and New Zealand.[24]

The case of Japanese participation in the School might help shed some light on its effects. Japanese students have been attending for a number of years, and several have achieved high standards of playing ability and have absorbed many of the nuances of Irish culture. In 2001, a party of fifteen students – interestingly, from the Japanese branch of CCÉ – attended the School, and in September 2001 a souvenir of their visit was issued in Tokyo. This is a typical example of their experiences:

> This year was my third time to participate in the School in Miltown. During the previous two years, I danced and danced without considering my strength but this time I took it relatively easy (or perhaps I just ran out of strength). This year, I chose the old style set dancing class, which is a 'deep' and 'rare' field (at least in my opinion). I learned much more than I expected and my ideas about set dancing have changed somewhat (I'll be talking in more detail about this at workshops and other opportunities). The size of the class, a little less than 20 people, was ideal, as it allowed us to interact with each other and our teacher, Mr Larry Lynch. I'll go to Miltown again next year, so I have to start earning my airfare![25]

The School has similar generally informal links with Irish traditional music associations in a number of overseas cities, including Milwaukee (USA), Odense (Denmark), Riga (Latvia) and Hamburg (Germany), as well as the link with the Scottish festival *Ceolas*. In addition, the well-known banjo player and musical authority Mick Moloney brings a group of American visitors each year to the School.

The degree to which overseas students take in the underlying philosophy of the School will depend on their level of participation and their language capability. Undoubtedly, fluent English speakers – the language used in teaching and that spoken by the majority of students – are more likely to absorb the School's core values.

Through the various forums devoted to Irish music, the Internet provides a convenient method of monitoring the attitudes and opinions of the contemporary global Irish music community to the School. The most well-established forum is Ir-Trad, whose contributors appear to cover the whole spectrum of Irish music, from the expert to the novice, from the casual listener to the most devoted practitioner. Around the middle of the year, Ir-Trad will contain many messages relating to the School. Prior to the event, these tend to concern arrangements for meeting fellow musicians. Following the event, the focus is on reporting personal experiences, followed by often lengthy discussions, particularly about the effectiveness of teaching. Although the groups are not mutually exclusive in membership, one group of correspondents will report and discuss their experiences as students, while another group will exchange memories of the many sessions attended.

Although Ir-Trad confirms the global extent of the School's reach to both students and sessioners, it is difficult to deduce tangible evidence of the School's effect on the musical performance of those attending. However, the ongoing discussions of style, use of ornamentation and detailed discussions on the musicians and practices of the past suggest that many contributors are making a conscious attempt to operate within the tradition. Certainly, irrespective of which camp correspondents fall into, it appears that, in general, both students and sessioners share at least the fundamental tenets of the School's underpinning philosophy, which, of course, is not unique to the School. However, it is hard to say whether the Ir-Trad group are drawn to the School because they perceive it as a place to meet those of a like mind or whether their views have been influenced, directly or indirectly, by the School.

In general, the dual nature and sheer size of the School make it hard to evaluate its precise role in the regeneration of Irish traditional music. Many who come to Miltown come simply to enjoy the *craic*, either as active or passive participants, and not to attend any of its educational events, other than perhaps the odd recital. As the various classes are run simultaneously, even the most diligent students can participate in only one class per year, although they may attend a good percentage of the official supporting events (recitals, lectures, *céilíthe*, etc.) and participate in the informal sessions.

In the specific case of the *uilleann* pipes, the School certainly appears to have had far reaching effects. Always a rare breed before the last three decades of the twentieth century, pipers do not appear to have played a major role in the music of the *clachans* of west Clare. Although Garret Barry and Willie Clancy achieved great fame, both were unusual figures in their own times and rightly hold a special place in the pantheon of piping gods. Barry was an inspirational figure for Willie Clancy, who, in turn, was highly influential for later pipers and was a major influence in Ireland's piping renaissance. As a result of its historic role as the first major school of Irish music and its ties with NPU, it can be truly claimed that the School has played a vital role in the effort to restore the country's piping traditions.

* * *

The decision to change the status of the ad hoc committee to that of a limited company in 1988 might be viewed as one that would reduce its community status. But, in truth, the Willie Clancy Summer School has never been solely a local community-based organisation, and representation from the local community has always been matched by that from outside elements: initially CCÉ, NPU from year two on, and, latterly, Brook's Academy. There has never been any mechanism for election to the committee by popular mandate, and from the outset the organising committee has been simply an informal coalescence of like-minded people with an agreed objective. It is the shared appreciation of the importance of a specific culture that bonds visitors to the School and has engendered such a strong relationship between students, musicians, the residents and the local music culture. It is a bond that transcends commercial considerations and has helped to maintain the unique community that is the Willie Clancy Summer School. It is also a bond that has enabled thousands of non-Clare musicians to help maintain cultural forms that otherwise would have been outside their experience and which, in spite of their apparent strength, might have been lost, as in less fortunate parts of Ireland.

In the final analysis, there is little or no difference between the School being controlled by the former self-elected committee or by the directors of a company. The mandate for the Willie Clancy Summer School is not the popular vote, but popular support.

There is no way that an event such as the School could hope to emulate the total integration of culture and community experienced in the *clachan*. However, the organisers of the School have built on the camaraderie that had developed between local and visiting musicians in the decade before Willie's death. By its recognition of the primacy of the musician, singer and dancer in setting the standards for the musical community, the School has helped to maintain much of the ethos of the long-gone communities that fostered the tradition. Paradoxically, by introducing regiments of young people to the music, many of whom have little or no connection with rural Ireland, it has helped to disseminate the ethos to an unparalleled extent.

With its reliance on a set of cultural practices that have, by a quirk of fate, survived the disintegration of the society in which they were developed and practised, the School is an anachronism in contemporary Ireland. It was born on the conviction of its founders that the values embodied in these practices would be of lasting benefit to the youth of late twentieth century Ireland – a conviction that has been endorsed by its continued growth over more than three decades.

As to its long-term survival, only time will tell whether such practices will continue to be valued in the rigours of the apparently increasingly competitive and money-orientated society of the twenty-first century.

Notes to Chapter 5

1   Section 2:1, *Promoting the Music Market*, a document prepared by the School's directors to support a funding application; also part of the company's articles of association.

2   Full-time students are those who pay for a full week's activities, whereas part-time students are those who enrol on a day-to-day basis. The latter method is common only in dance classes, and the organisers made a strenuous, but not always successful, attempt to limit this practice in 2001.

3   For example, the author became aware of the School in 1973 by word of mouth as a result of being involved in folk-clubs and regularly attending Irish music sessions in London pubs. It was then, and remains to this day, 'the place to go' if you have an aspiration to be involved in playing or dancing to Irish music.

4   *Promoting the Music Market*. The independent survey was carried out by Shane Malone; see *Conceptualisation and Transformation in the Culture of Traditional Music in Clare: A Study of the Willie Clancy School*, unpublished thesis, University College Galway, 1996.

5   CCÉ official website (www.comhaltas.com), 2002.

6   Recorded conversation between Nicholas Carolan and Barry Taylor, Dublin, 24 April 1998.

7   Unrecorded conversations between Darach Ó Catháin and Barry Taylor, Leeds, around 1975.

8   For a discussion on the use of musical notation, see Breandán Breathnach, 'The Use of Notation in the Transmission of Irish Folk Music', in Seán Potts, Terry Moylan and Liam McNulty, eds, 'The Man and His Music', *Dal gCais*, vol. 1 (1972), pp. 92f.

9   For further information, see Nicholas Carolan, *A Harvest Saved: Francis O'Neill and Irish Music in Chicago* (Cork: Ossian, 1997).

10 See Breandán Breathnach, 'The Use of Notation', p. 99.

11 See Micheál Ó Súilleabháin's analysis of the playing of Tommy Potts in 'Crossroads or Twin Track? Innovation and Tradition in Irish Traditional Music', *Crosbhealach an Cheoil*, p. 175. It should be pointed out that several contributors cited Potts' playing to prove the opposite!

12 Editorial, *An Píobaire*, no. 2/36 (1987), p. 1.

13 It should be noted that CCÉ has extensive teaching programmes in other countries, notably the USA and the UK, but also in areas that do not have a significant Irish population, such as Japan and countries of the Benelux region.

14 Recorded conversation between Harry Hughes and Barry Taylor, Mullagh, County Clare, 1 June 1998.

15 Recorded conversation between Finbar Boyle and Barry Taylor, Dublin, 23 April 1998. Since these comments were recorded, several of the town's pubs have closed and a number have undergone or are undergoing significant modernisation, including Friel's pub, which has now passed out of family ownership.

16 From Alexander Wilson, *The Culture of Nature: North American Landscape from Disney to Exxon Valdez* (Oxford: Blackwell, 1992); quoted by Patrick Duffy, 'Conflicts in Heritage and Tourism', in U. Kockel, ed., *Culture, Tourism and Development: The Case of Ireland* (Liverpool: University Press, 1994), p. 77.

17 To the author's knowledge, only one such detailed study of the area's potential for cultural tourism has been undertaken. See Deirdre Hughes, *Small Town or World Capital?*, unpublished dissertation as part of BA (Hons), University of Wales Institute Cardiff, April 2001.

18 For example, 'immigrant' musicians are to the fore at most of the organised pub sessions that take place around the year.

19 Edward M. Said, *Culture and Imperialism* (New York: Vantage, 1994), pp. 1f.

20 See Eric Hobsbawm and Terence Ranger, eds, *The Invention of Tradition* (Cambridge: Cambridge University Press, 1992).

21 1995 – a joint RTÉ and BBC production; written and presented by Micheál Ó Súilleabháin and produced by Phillip King.

22 *Late, Late Show Special*, RTÉ, February 1995.

23 The proceedings of the conference are available in *Crosbhealach an Cheoil* (*Crossroads Conference of* 1996) – *Tradition and Change in Irish Traditional Music*, edited by Fintan Vallely, Hammy Hamilton, Eithne Vallely and Liz Doherty.

24 Precise figures are difficult to arrive at. The numbers attending organised events have been estimated on gross figures, making allowance for the tendency for students to make regular return visits. The numbers of informal visitors is based on estimates from the organisers.

25 Tamiko Oyama, from 'Miltown Report', CCÉ Japan newsletter, edited by Megumi Murakami; September 2001.

Saturday

IT'S THE FINAL day of the School, and back in St Joseph's School the fiddle players are coming to terms with the fact. Since Monday, Brendan McGlinchey's class has altered considerably, taking on a definite North American flavour. The man from Boston is still here, while the girl with the fiery technique is revealed to be from Maine. A girl from Montreal and another New Englander have been added. Most of the younger players have drifted off to other, perhaps less advanced, classes. The stresses and strains of a week's hard playing and living are showing on some faces, and Brendan admits to feeling a little tired.

'I want you to listen to some music this morning,' says Brendan and plays a recording of Irish fiddle music made in the twenties or thirties. The man from New England says, 'Wow, that sounds just like French-Canadian music.'

Brendan then plays a recording of a Shetland fiddle player. 'It'll help to improve your own playing if you listen to a wide variety of different musicians, because you can hear something different in each one.'

The tension of the first morning has disappeared, and the members of the class seem relaxed in each other's company. An Englishman recounts a story from a session that he was in the previous day: 'Connie Connell was playing, and he went out for a couple of minutes. When he came back, he went as if to sit on a fiddle that had been placed on one of the chairs. A load of people jumped up to stop him, and he just straightened up and broke into laughter: "That always gets them." What a character.' The class swap stories of the week, and Brendan is happy to listen quietly, knowing that the School has worked it's usual magic for yet another group.

* * *

Elsewhere, Sean McNamara is coping on his own, as Liam O'Connor is covering for an absent teacher in another class. Again, the make-up of the class has changed since Monday morning, with some new faces replacing those who have left for other classes. However, big improvements in playing technique are obvious when the group begin to play. 'Try that "Terry Teahan's Polka",' urges Sean, and the group take up their instruments. One small girl asks Sean to tune up her fiddle before starting. In the course of the week, the class has got through ten tunes – no small achievements for a group of students whose abilities were fairly limited at the start.

* * *

Of all the classes, perhaps that of Martin Hayes has remained the most constant. During the week, in addition to learning some new tunes and absorbing some of Martin's techniques, discussion has ranged widely over all aspects of traditional music. In the final session, the class is anxious to find out Martin's views on the future of Irish music. 'You know, we can never recreate what has gone before, all the social, economic and political circumstances that provided the background for people like my father and Paddy Canny. Whatever motivated Junior Crehan to produce his music has gone for ever. We have to find something from inside ourselves now. Perhaps the music needs more thought, more input from a wider range of artistic endeavour.'

Martin compares the development of Irish music with that of jazz. 'When those guys were first playing jazz, it was the expression of a people who had been downtrodden and ignored by the society that they lived in. It was their way of expressing their feelings and ideas. Nowadays, the emotion has gone from jazz and we are just left with the technique. Every college in America has a department of jazz studies, as well as classical music, and the students can play all the solos that John Coltrane ever played. But they haven't

Tea break for fiddle and accordion tutors, St Joseph's Secondary School, 2001.

Marie Power from Ennis, County Clare (centre), with her fellow students in Martin Hayes' fiddle class, 2001.

gone through the process of discovery that Coltrane and those guys went through. In some ways, I think that Irish music is heading in this direction.'

Someone mentions that the music has become very dislocated from the dance. Martin agrees. 'I know that I play very slowly – probably no one plays as slowly as me!' He laughs and demonstrates with his version of 'The Morning Star', tapping his feet in his characteristic way to the rhythm of the reel. 'But whatever I play, no matter how slowly, it's always in rhythm; I'm always thinking of the dance. I played for years with the Tulla Céilí Band and loved it, so I don't separate the music in my mind.'

Martin is asked whether he plays in many sessions. 'Well, perhaps not so many, but I like to play in sessions with people I know. I'm not so craving for a session that I need to scour the town to find one. In some ways, I think that sessions have been quite bad for the music. You know, they make people feel very anxious about their playing: do I know enough tunes, is this person sitting next to me a better player than me, will I disgrace myself, etc.?'

So the week finally slows to a halt. Many of the class ask Martin for his autograph – autographed copies of his notes for the recently re-released CD of his father's great old recording seem to be a popular choice. A number of the younger members of the class ask to be photographed with Martin, who laughingly agrees, seeming a little embarrassed at the request.

Over 400 fiddle students and teachers give a mighty cheer outside St Joseph's Secondary School, Spanish Point, 2001.

* * *

Outside in the bright sunshine, little knots of students say their farewells. Some will come again next year and for many years afterwards. Some will, perhaps, never return to west Clare. All will depart at least a little wiser for the experience.